Tax-Savvy Solo

Smart Strategies for Solo Entrepreneurs

by
Well-Being Publishing

To You,

Thank you!

Contents

Introduction:
Navigating the Landscape of Solo Entrepreneurship and Taxes

Embarking on the journey of solo entrepreneurship is simultaneously exhilarating and daunting. With every step towards building your dream, the looming complexity of taxes can seem like a hurdle that's both mystifying and unavoidable. Fear not, as this guide is crafted to demystify the tax maze, steering you through the twists and turns of fiscal responsibilities and smart planning. Consider this your operating manual for tackling taxes head-on, transforming them from a source of anxiety into a strategic tool for your financial empowerment. You're not just running a business; you're mastering the fine art of keeping more of your hard-earned money in your pocket and away from unnecessary tax expenditures. We'll be your guide in laying a sturdy foundation for managing your tax obligations, ensuring compliance, and revealing opportunities to maximize your savings. So let's sharpen those pencils and dive into the world of solo entrepreneurship and taxes—navigating these waters hand-in-hand ensures smoother sailing ahead.

Chapter 1:
Understanding the Tax System:
A Primer for Solo Entrepreneurs

Embarking on the solo entrepreneurial journey brings its own set of challenges and rewards, not least of which is understanding the often intimidating labyrinth of the tax system. It's crucial to start with a solid foundation, discerning the myriad of options for structuring your enterprise, and grasp the implications each structure has on your taxes. Think of the tax system as a game where knowing the rules can provide you with legitimate advantages. Whether you're contemplating the benefits of an LLC or wondering about S Corp election, remember these aren't just bureaucratic hoops to jump through; they're strategic choices that affect your financial health. Next up are the tax obligations that come with being self-employed, from self-employment tax to the rhythm of estimated tax payments. While the details of these will unfold in the coming pages, consider this chapter the map that helps chisel out your path through the tax terrain. By the end, you'll be better equipped to not just meet your obligations but also to wield the tax system to your benefit as a savvy solo entrepreneur.

Structuring Your Solo Enterprise: LLC, S Corp, and Other Considerations

Diving into the architectural makeup of your business carries more weight than just its name or logo; it's about finding the perfect balance between legal protections, financial savvy, and ease of management. When pondering the question of whether to set up an LLC (Limited Liability Company), tap into the sleek world of S Corps, or maybe even something else, consider this: each structure holds the key to distinctive tax advantages and obligations uniquely aligned with your business goals. An LLC, for instance, keeps things simple and offers a protective shield for your personal assets without the fuss of corporate formalities, whereas an S Corp could unlock potential savings on self-employment taxes, albeit with stricter guidelines to adhere to. Remember, it's not just about paying taxes; it's about structuring your enterprise in a way that cushions your wallet while ensuring you're playing by the rules. Your enterprise is not just your livelihood; it's your magnum opus. Frame it correctly, and you create a remarkably robust platform for your entrepreneurial symphony to resonate from.

Advantages and Disadvantages of Different Business Structures It's a decision that could steer the ship of your small enterprise through calm or choppy tax waters: Choosing the right business structure. You're not just picking out a name or deciding between sleek office space vs. the comfy home setup; you're laying down the foundation that determines how much you'll pay in taxes, the type and volume of paperwork you'll manage, and the personal liability you'll carry. So roll up your sleeves, and let's break down the pros and cons of the common structures you might be considering.

Starting with the simplest form, the **sole proprietorship**, it tends to be attractive because it's easy and economical to set up. You and your business are essentially one and the same for tax purposes, which means less red tape. However, keep in mind that any debts or lawsuits aimed at your business are coming straight for your personal assets. Additionally, when it comes to self-employment taxes, you're on the hook for the full amount.

Next, let's talk about the **Partnership**. If your business is a duo or more, a partnership could be right up your alley. This is where things start to get a bit more complex tax-wise—partnerships file an information return, but don't pay income taxes. Instead, profits pass through to partners who then report on their individual returns. The con here? Like sole proprietorships, partners can be personally liable for business debts.

Perhaps you've considered an **LLC (Limited Liability Company)**. It's got flexibility that might make you swoon; you can opt for it to be taxed like a sole proprietorship, partnership, or even a corporation. And here's the kicker—in most cases, your personal assets get a shield from business issues. But let's not sugarcoat it; it often Requires more paperwork and sometimes additional state-level taxes.

On to the big kid on the block, the **C-Corporation**. Separation is the name of the game here; C-Corps are independent entities that pay their own taxes. They can raise capital through stock sales, which could be a big plus if you're looking to expand. Drawbacks? Well, the tax complexities leapfrog here, and you could get slapped with double taxation—once at the corporate level and again on dividends you receive.

The **S-Corporation** might be seen as the best of both worlds. It offers some of the C-Corp benefits but with pass-through taxation. You can pay yourself a "reasonable" salary and possibly save on self-employment taxes with earnings distributions. Sounds dreamy, right? But tread carefully; the IRS keeps a close eye on what you define as 'reasonable', and there are strict rules on who can be shareholders and what type of stock you can issue.

Moving on to the little-known, but sometimes handy, **Cooperative**. Members of cooperatives can get the tax benefit of deducting business expenses before income is allocated among them. They also have less personal liability and can influence management decisions. However, setting up and running a co-op involves a complex organizational structure and operating on consensus, which isn't everyone's cup of tea.

If you're leaning towards simplicity and saving on taxes, don't overlook the humble **Sole Proprietorship**. It's still on the table, especially for small, low-risk businesses. The boon here is the potential to reduce taxes by offsetting business losses against your other personal income—a strategy not to be underestimated. But, it's important to remember, you'll be wearing all the hats, and juggling all the balls, with no one to pass them to.

Now let's circle back to those **Partnerships**. There's something to be said for sharing the burden of business decisions and debts. And while each partner's share of the profits is taxable income, that can go both ways—you can also share the losses for tax benefit. Keep in mind though, profits must be divvied up according to the partnership agreement, which means you've got to really trust and play fair with your business partners.

With an **LLC**, you might feel like you've hit the sweet spot; especially if you're a fan of flexibility and keeping personal legal worries separate from your business. There's also the benefit of avoiding the pesky double taxation scenario of a C Corp. But, don't let the fanfare drown out the potential downsides, like the additional fees and state taxes that can sneak up on you.

The **C-Corporation** structure may have its complexities, but it comes with perks for the tax-savvy. Benefit from business expense deductions, and if you're making it rain, corporate tax rates might be more favorable than personal tax rates. But, the potential for that double taxation sting hasn't gone anywhere; your wallet might feel the pinch both from corporate income taxes and from personal taxes on dividends.

When you're considering an **S-Corporation** as your go-to, you're eyeing the advantage of pass-through taxation while still reaping the rewards of corporate life. This could mean significant self-employment tax savings compared to sole proprietorships or partnerships. But keep your wits about you; the S-Corp comes with eligibility requirements and stricter IRS scrutiny. Long story short, play by the rules or be prepared to justify your moves.

Within the sphere of **Cooperatives**, it's unique how they bolster solidarity among members and their ability to influence the business. Profits can be distributed on a patronage basis rather than on investment, which could create a more equitable structure. Yet, cooperating might not be your forte, and the complexity of such a setup shouldn't be underestimated—making it a less popular choice for solo entrepreneurs.

Choosing a **Sole Proprietorship** for its ease of setup and low cost isn't a poor choice for the right business. Its straightforward tax reporting can be a major plus. Yet, it bears repeating—the risk to your personal assets is undeniable and should be weighed heavily against the simplicity it offers.

And remember, no matter the structure, each has its own nuanced impact on your retirement plans, health insurance deductions, and the way you'll approach an IRS audit. The key is to evaluate how your chosen entity will not just coexist, but thrive with your specific business strategy, personal assets, and future objectives.

So, there you have it. Whether you're a lone gunslinger in the business world or aiming to build a small empire, the structure you choose can have a profound impact on your tax outlook. Consider carefully, consult with a professional if needed, and pick the structure that aligns with your business goals, risk tolerance, and financial aspirations. After all, your business is more than your livelihood—it's a reflection of your vision and hard work.

Tax Obligations for the Self-Employed: What You Need to Know

As you journey through the world of solo entrepreneurship, it's crucial to grip the reins of your tax obligations with confidence. You're not just wearing the hat of a trailblazing entrepreneur; you're also the payroll department, HR, and yes, the tax specialist. Understanding tax liabilities is more than a necessity—it's a stride towards empowerment. As a self-employed maverick, you'll deal with taxes that traditional employees often never see, like self-employment tax, which covers your due Social Security and Medicare taxes. But don't let that dampen your spirits; with every expense that rolls in, remember, there's a potential tax deduction lying in wait. You'll need to wrap your head around estimated tax payments, ensuring you pay the IRS in timely installments to avoid those dreaded penalties. This isn't your typical 9-to-5's W-2 form; this is the ongoing puzzle of managing your financial picture quarterly. So, set aside that portion of your earnings, track your business expenses meticulously, and let's turn the complexity of tax obligations into a strategic game where you're always aiming for high score—they're not just mundane numbers, they're the lifeblood of your business's financial health.

Self-Employment Tax Basics ...Navigating the murkiness of self-employment tax isn't exactly the thrilling part of entrepreneurship. Yet, understanding these basics is absolutely critical to ensure you're not leaving money on the table or, on the flip side, getting on the wrong side of tax laws. As a solo entrepreneur, you're probably familiar with income tax, but self-employment tax is a different beast — one that warrants our undivided attention.

The concept is straightforward. When you work for someone else, your employer pays half of your Social Security and Medicare taxes, while the other half is withheld from your paycheck. However, as the boss of your own show, you're responsible for both halves. This is what's known as self-employment tax, which comprises 12.4% for Social Security and 2.9% for Medicare, totaling 15.3% on your net earnings.

Feeling the pinch yet? Well, consider this: self-employment tax applies only to your business profit — that is, your earnings after deducting business expenses. So, keeping meticulous records isn't just good practice for organization; it directly impacts your taxable income. Chapter 2 will dive deeper into effective record-keeping.

Now brace yourself for a bit of good news. You aren't taxed on every penny you earn. The IRS generously allows you to deduct half of your self-employment tax when calculating your adjusted gross income. This adjustment doesn't affect your net earnings concerning self-employment tax, but it does lower your income tax.

Understanding the contribution limits is also crucial. For Social Security tax, there's an income cap — you pay into it only up to a certain amount of earnings each year. Luckily, Medicare tax doesn't have such a cap, but higher earners may be subjected to an additional Medicare tax. Savvy planning here can help you anticipate when these taxes kick in.

The IRS isn't known for its leniency, and not paying your self-employment tax can lead to a path of penalties. That's why making estimated tax payments quarterly can keep you in good standing — yes, it's an arduous task, but Chapter 1 covers the "how" and "when" to save you headaches.

When does this tax apply, you ask? If you earn $400 or more from self-employment within the year, the clock starts ticking on self-employment taxes. That's a low threshold, so it catches many part-timers or hobbyists who might not consider themselves typical business owners.

If you also work as an employee while running your solo gig, your total Social Security taxes need some extra calculation. Why? Because there's a ceiling on how much you have to contribute each year, and wages from employment count toward that limit. This could work in your favor if you've hit the maximum with your earned income.

A common faux pas is mistaking self-employment tax for income tax. They are separate entities — while self-employment tax pays for Social Security and Medicare, income tax is based on your total income. However, paying self-employment tax doesn't mean you can give income tax the cold shoulder; they're both due to Uncle Sam.

You're not alone in this journey. If self-employment tax calculations evoke a headache, software and professionals are there to guide you. Chapter 10 will guide you through hiring professionals, ensuring every dime you spend on their services is worthwhile — consider them an investment in peace of mind.

Remember, as self-employed, your tax situation is unique. You may be subject to additional taxes like the Net Investment Income Tax, or you may be eligible for tax credits specific to your situation. It's vital to stay informed on these nuances to effectively manage your obligations.

Having a year-round tax mindset is key. Don't wait until tax season to think about self-employment taxes. By tracking your expenses, income, and estimated taxes throughout the year, you're not just prepared; you're empowered. Future chapters, especially Chapter 4 on Strategic Tax Planning, are dedicated to this mindset.

If you're a visual learner, draw up graphs or charts reflecting your estimated payments and expected tax liability. Sometimes seeing it on paper makes the abstract more concrete — a visual manifesto of where your hard-earned money is going.

Let's not forget, the IRS offers a wealth of information, and several resources can assist in demystifying self-employment taxes. Appendix A is packed with tools and resources to help you navigate the tumultuous seas of tax compliance.

Embrace the fact that self-employment tax is a sign of your success. Every payment is a reminder that you are living the dream — being your own boss, carving your own path. With each calculated payment, you are declaring your independence and shouldering the responsibility of your accomplishments.

As we press on through this book, remember that self-employment tax isn't just an obligation; it's a testament to your entrepreneurial spirit. By mastering the essentials of self-employment tax, you're laying down the financial foundation to thrive. With the right knowledge, every tax decision you make can contribute to your long-term business success and personal prosperity.

Estimated Tax Payments: How and When Diving into the world of estimated tax payments can be like unraveling a knitted sweater – if you pull the right strings, things will unfold smoothly, but a single snag can complicate the whole process. Mastering the ebb and flow of quarterly payments is essential for any solo entrepreneur. It's not just about staying compliant; it's about the peace of mind that comes with keeping the IRS at bay.

Let's clarify one thing right off the bat: if you expect to owe at least $1,000 in taxes for the year after subtracting your withholding and credits, then you need to make estimated tax payments. This is the IRS's way of ensuring that you pay as you go. For traditional employees, employers handle withholding. For the self-employed, you're effectively wearing all the hats, including that of the tax collector.

Estimated taxes are typically paid in four installments. The due dates are April 15, June 15, September 15, and January 15 of the following year. If any of these dates fall on a weekend or holiday, the due date is the next business day. Mark these dates on your calendar as they are as important as client deadlines.

To figure out how much you'll owe, you can use last year's tax return as a guide. The IRS offers a safe harbor rule: if you pay 100% of the tax you owed the previous year (or 110% if you're a high earner), you should avoid penalties, even if you end up owing more. This is like setting cruise control to avoid speeding tickets.

Now, calculating your taxes doesn't require a crystal ball, but it does require vigilance. You can use Form 1040-ES, which includes worksheets to help estimate your taxes. Incorporate all your streams of income, and don't forget to consider deductions and credits you plan to claim. Think of it as giving your wallet a preemptive health checkup.

Life and business are anything but static, and your estimated payments can reflect that. Perhaps the second quarter was surprisingly good, or the third a bit slow – adjust your estimated payments accordingly. While overpayments can result in a refund, underpayments could lead to penalties. So it's a balancing act you'll want to get right.

When it comes time to pay, you've got options. The IRS offers electronic payment options through the Electronic Federal Tax Payment System (EFTPS), where you can schedule payments and even pay from your smartphone. There's the old-school approach of mailing a check with a voucher from Form 1040-ES, or you can pay online, by phone, or through a mobile app using Direct Pay.

To avoid late payments, which can incur interest and penalties, consider setting up electronic reminders, or even better, automatic payments through EFTPS. This is one less thing to worry about and ensures that your taxes are paid on time.

If you come to the end of the year and realize you've significantly underestimated your income – don't panic. Increase your final payment to cover the difference. Alternatively, if you overestimate, slow down on that final payment. Remember, estimated taxes are just that – estimates. Adjust as you go, and you'll stay on the IRS's good side.

To simplify your life, keep good records. You've heard it before, but it bears repeating because it will save you enormous headaches. Recording income and expenses in real-time, or as close to it as possible, paints an accurate picture of your tax situation. Strong records make strong estimates.

In the event that you do make a mistake, the IRS might penalize you for underpayment of estimated tax. However, you may get these penalties reduced or even waived if you can show reasonable cause for underestimating your tax, or if this is the first time you're facing this hiccup. Being proactive and communicative with the IRS can often work in your favor.

If your income is heavily seasonal, you can make unequal payments through the 'annualized income installment' method. This method tailors your payments to your income flow, potentially reducing penalties for underpayment in slower income periods. This is like throttle control for a bumpy financial ride.

Keep in mind, if you also work as an employee and have taxes withheld from your paycheck, you can increase your withholding to cover the taxes due from your side gig. This can be an alternative way to address the estimated tax payment if managing quarterly payments feels overwhelming.

Battling through a tough financial period? If you can't make a payment, still file the estimated tax form and pay as much as you can. This minimizes penalties and sends a message to the IRS that you're not ignoring your responsibilities. Arrange a payment plan with the IRS if you need to; they're more flexible than you might think.

Ultimately, a disciplined approach to estimated taxes can be your fiscal superpower. Embrace the predictability of quarterly payments to avoid year-end surprises. Smooth out your financial path and watch your business thrive, free from the looming shadow of tax mishaps. This aspect of financial planning isn't just routine – it's a cornerstone of empowered entrepreneurship.

Chapter 2:
Essential Record-Keeping for Tax Success

Having peeled back the layers of the tax system in our primer, let's shift gears into the nuts and bolts of your tax success: meticulous record-keeping. Remember, every receipt, invoice, and financial statement is a piece of the puzzle that is your tax profile. You might ask, "Why keep such detailed records?" Well, they're not just the foundation for bulletproof tax returns; they're your roadmap to identifying every deduction and credit you're entitled to. Setting up a lean, mean accounting system isn't just about compliance; it's about transforming what could be an entrepreneurial headache into a well-oiled machine that can save you a bundle. We're diving into the do's and don'ts of documenting your income and expenses, crafting a tapestry of best practices that will have you tracking deductions like a pro. From stunningly simple spreadsheets to state-of-the-art software, it's time to curate your financial narrative—keeping it as accurate as it is insightful. Embrace the financial storyteller in you, and let your records recount your business journey—one where every chapter spells out tax success.

Setting Up Effective Accounting Systems

Let's get into the nitty-gritty of shaping an accounting system that's the belle of the ball among its peers. Think of your accounting system as the silent sentinel of your financial realm, tirelessly keeping track of every penny that rolls in and out. Establishing this financial fortress isn't just smart; it's your lifeline to stress-free tax times.

An organized, reliable system helps keep your financial house in order, so let's build one that can stand up to the demands of solo entrepreneurship. It's not just about being ready for tax time; it's about gaining insight into the very heart of your business cash flow, understanding where your money is spinning its wheels and where it's fueling your growth.

To start off, you'll need to decide whether you're going the DIY route with software solutions or enlisting the help of a professional. Technology has given us tools like accounting software that can automate almost every aspect of financial management. They're typically user-friendly and come filled to the brim with features specifically crafted for the solo entrepreneur. But if you're more inclined to focus on your trade rather than trade spreadsheets, a professional might be your best bet.

Let's dive into the software first. Your pick should be a platform that's not just a flash in the pan – it's got to be reputable and robust. Think scalability, think intuitive design, and definitely think about security. Do some digging, read reviews, and maybe take a few for a test spin with their free trials. The aim here is to find a tool that you're comfortable with, that you can scale with, and that can produce the reports that you – and Uncle Sam – will need at a click's notice.

Bank accounts and your accounting software should be akin to dance partners; they've got to work in harmony. Set up business bank accounts that can easily synchronize with your chosen software, ensuring a smooth flow of information and helping eliminate manual entry errors – those nasty buggers can really throw a wrench in your gears.

Next, we can't forget the importance of categorizing transactions. This isn't just busywork; it's about painting a clear picture of your financial landscape. Set up categories that reflect the nature of your expenses and income. When tax time rolls around, having things broken down neatly can save you hours of head scratching.

Income tracking keeps the lights on, so treat it with kid gloves. Record every sale, gig, or payment with all the care of an artist finishing a masterpiece. You'll want to know not just how much you made, but where it came from — this can pinpoint which parts of your business are the real breadwinners.

Expense tracking is the yin to income tracking's yang. Developing a habit of recording expenses as they happen can save you a mountain of time and a molehill of stress. Everything from the coffee you bought for a client meet-up to the ink for your printer – if it's for the business, it gets recorded. Missed expenses mean missed deductions, and that's just leaving money on the table.

A word to the wise: tie up your loose receipts. Physical or digital, these snippets are proof of your business expenditures, and you'll be grateful for each one when deductions are on the line. Find a system for organizing them that you'll stick to, maybe it's a cloud service or an old-fashioned accordion file – whatever floats your entrepreneurial boat.

Now, let's talk about reconciliations. This is your fail-safe check that your records are on point. Periodically, you'll want to match your records with your bank statements. This ensures that what you say you have and what you actually have are singing the same tune. It's a bit like detective work, but instead of looking for whodunnits, you're ensuring there are no "what-did-I-miss-its."

And speaking of checks, create a regular schedule for managing your accounting tasks. Whether it's daily, weekly, or monthly, the key is consistency. Setting aside time in your calendar makes sure that these essential tasks get the attention they deserve. Think of it as an appointment with the future success of your business.

As you nurture your business, your accounting system should evolve with it. Stay attuned to its needs, and don't shy away from upgrading or customizing your system as your business landscape changes. Flexibility and adaptability can be the allies that help you sail smoothly through growth spurts and changing tides.

Don't neglect the insights your accounting system can offer. Beyond the nuts and bolts of tracking and reporting, it's a treasure trove of data that can help make informed business decisions. Regularly review your financial statements — the Profit and Loss, the Balance Sheet, and the Cash Flow Statement. They can tell you stories about the health of your business that nothing else can.

Last but not least, while your accounting system is your fortress, remember that it's also your stepping stone toward informed collaboration with tax professionals. When the times come – and they will – that you need to bring in the big guns for advice or in preparation for tax submissions, having an immaculate record-keeping system will make their work more efficient, more accurate, and probably cheaper for you.

So, arm yourself with a robust accounting system, and you're not just preparing for tax season; you're unlocking the potential of your business. You're setting up your future self for success and ensuring the taxman becomes an ally, not an adversary. Here's to a system that stands as a testament to your dedication and entrepreneurship – your quiet guardian in the realm of profit and loss.

Documenting Income and Expenses: Best Practices

Keeping an immaculate record of income and expenses isn't just a necessity for tax time; it's your financial dashboard. To nail this, ensure every dollar earned and spent is tracked. This means issuing invoices for all sales or services and keeping them aligned with bank statements. Equally, log every expense, whether it's a new laptop or a business lunch - these receipts are golden. A dedicated business credit card for expenses simplifies tracking, and software apps that sync with your bank account are lifesavers here. Don't forget, date and categorize each transaction - this attention to detail is vital for maximizing deductions and making future financial planning a breeze. Remember, an auditor's favorite word is 'proof,' so let's make sure your records speak volumes of your professionalism and preparedness.

Tracking Deductions Throughout the Year

Imagine hitting the end of the financial year and, rather than scrambling to find receipts and tally expenses, you're completely relaxed. This sense of ease isn't just wishful thinking—it's what tracking deductions throughout the year can bring. The most adept solo entrepreneurs know that managing taxes is an ongoing process—not just a frantic April activity.

Meticulous record-keeping is the backbone of your financial peace. And by keeping a close eye on potential deductions as they occur, you simplify your year-end process and often uncover hidden savings. So let's dive into the habits that can make this dream a reality. First, get a robust accounting system in place. Software that automates expense tracking is invaluable, creating logs of transactions which can be easily categorized and recalled when needed.

Once you have a system running, make it a habit to review and categorize transactions weekly. This approach not only helps with budgeting and managing cash flow but it also ensures that come tax time, you've got a detailed account of deductible expenses at your fingertips.

Be exhaustive in your categorization. Don't leave a transaction untagged, and if you're unsure whether something is deductible, flag it for further review. Sometimes, a small expense you wouldn't think twice about could be a legitimate business deduction, such as mileage for a client visit or a portion of your home internet bill if you work remotely.

Speaking of which, understanding the nuances of home office deductions is critical. Know which expenses count—like a dedicated office space's rent or mortgage interest—and track them separately. Pro tip: Take photographs of your home office setup as documentation to validate your claim.

Don't forget the little things. A coffee with a client, a software subscription, or even the notebooks purchased for brainstorming sessions—these can all add up. Keeping digital or physical copies of receipts is a must. There are plenty of apps that can scan and store these for you, making them searchable and easily attachable to the corresponding ledger entries.

Car-related expenses often go untracked, but with the standard mileage rate or actual car expenses being deductible, keeping a mileage log can pay off. Whether it's a notebook in your glove compartment or a GPS-enabled app, tracking every business-related trip is a habit that could mean significant savings.

Don't pay for deductible expenses with cash if you can avoid it. Using a dedicated business credit or debit card creates an automatic transaction record. Cash transactions, while still legitimate, require more steadfast record-keeping and can be tougher to substantiate in case of an audit.

The big-ticket items - equipment, machinery, or furniture - often qualify for depreciation deductions or even a Section 179 immediate deduction. However, it's not the purchase but the use of these items in your business that determines their deductibility. Record the use date, and keep purchase receipts and a log of use to prove their business connection.

Charitable contributions made through your enterprise can be deductible. Whether it's a cash donation or an in-kind contribution, they should be acknowledged with proper documentation for tax purposes. Importantly, understand the limitations and requirements for these kinds of deductions to ensure they're done right.

Education and professional development are often overlooked deductions. Keep tabs on any courses, webinars, or literature that directly improve or are necessary for your current business operations. And yes, that does mean keeping a record of registration fees, related travel expenses, and event costs.

Even meals can be deductible, so long as they serve a business purpose. The recent tax law change has increased the deduction limit for business meals to 100% through 2022, if the meal is provided by a restaurant. Save those receipts and note the purpose of the meeting on them, as a memory jogger when tax time arrives.

Health insurance premiums, if you're self-employed, can be another major deductible expense. Tracking these premiums alongside your other medical costs throughout the year will make it easier to calculate the Self-Employed Health Insurance Deduction when you file your taxes.

Finally, consistently use a checklist to ensure you're not missing anything. With the myriad tasks a solo entrepreneur juggles, it's easy to overlook a potential deduction. A monthly run-through of a carefully considered checklist is like a safety net for your finances.

Remember, tracking deductions is a pivotal part of maximizing your business's financial health. In essence, it's about more than just saving money—it's about empowering you to make informed, strategic business decisions that bolster your enterprise all year round. So keep your eyes on the financial road ahead, and let's make this the year that tax time transitions from a stress-inducing scramble to a seamless step in your business journey.

Chapter 3:
Maximizing Deductions and Credits

The journey into the heart of your tax savings continues with an empowering dive into maximizing deductions and credits. If you've ever felt that twinge of excitement when finding money in an old jacket, prepare to multiply that feeling because we're about to uncover a treasure trove of financial benefits that are just waiting to lower your tax bill. Whether it's turning your home office into a deduction goldmine, ensuring you're squeezing every ounce of value from your health insurance premiums, or building your nest egg with savvy retirement account contributions, this chapter is your map to keeping more of your hard-earned cash. We'll not just slot in deductions here and there; we'll craft a strategic approach to claiming every credit that rightfully belongs to you, all while navigating the twists and turns of tax laws with confidence. Remember, each dollar saved in taxes through legitimate deductions and credits is a dollar that can be reinvested back into your business, your future, or simply enjoyed in the now. So let's get set to claim your rightful rewards and boost your financial health with the acumen of a tax-savvy entrepreneur.

Home Office Deduction: Requirements and Limitations

When you're running your business from home, every square foot can matter—not just for your productivity but also for your taxes. That's where the home office deduction comes into play, providing financial relief for entrepreneurs like ourselves who use part of our homes for business. If you're thinking this sounds like an area ripe for savings, you're spot-on.

First up, let's make clear what qualifies as a home office. It's not just any space where you occasionally check emails or take calls. This area must be used regularly and exclusively for conducting the business. That means your kitchen table won't cut it if you're also using it for family meals. If you've got a dedicated room or a partitioned area that's solely for business, that's more like it. The IRS wants to see clear boundaries.

But it's not just about having the right space; knowing how to calculate your deduction is crucial. There are two methods: the simplified option and the actual expense method. The simplified option is quick and straightforward, letting you deduct $5 per square foot of your home office, up to a maximum of 300 square feet. It's a breath of fresh air for those of us who prefer to steer clear of complicated calculations.

Now, let's talk about the actual expense method. It involves more math, but it can be worth it, especially if your home office is larger than 300 square feet or you have significant home-related expenses. You'll calculate your deduction based on the percentage of your home devoted to business use. This means tracking all home expenses, like mortgage interest, property taxes, utilities, repairs, and maintenance, then divvying up those costs between personal and business use.

Remember, standards for documentation are stringent. You can't just estimate; you need to back up your claims with receipts, bills, and records. This paper trail isn't just for proving expenses; it's a shield if the IRS knocks on your door with questions or concerns.

What about renters? Yes, you're in the game as well. You can still claim the home office deduction, using the same methods to calculate your write-off. Your rent, and even renter's insurance, can be part of the expenses that may qualify.

Moving on, there are limitations, folks. Your deduction can't exceed the gross income from your business minus other business expenses. So if your business isn't profitable yet, the home office deduction isn't going to generate a refund out of thin air.

Also, let's not overlook the importance of the home office deduction come time to sell. Depreciation comes into play here—overlooked by many. If you're claiming actual expenses, depreciation on the portion of your home used for the business can reduce your tax bill now. But remember, when you sell your home, you'll have to account for that depreciation, which might mean paying taxes on some of the proceeds from the sale. It's a balancing act.

Furthermore, the home office deduction is emblematic of the golden tax rule: use it, but don't abuse it. Exaggerating the size of your home office or slipping personal expenses into the mix can invite scrutiny. The IRS knows the average size of a home office; wildly deviating from this average can be a flag.

Is the home office deduction worth the potential scrutiny? Absolutely. Just ensure you're playing by the rules. Speak up in your records. Be meticulous. And remember, this deduction is there to reward you for the steps you've taken to carve out a part of your home for the noble pursuit of business. It's recognizing your dedication and investment.

There's a psychological boost as well. Claiming the home office deduction can reinforce the seriousness of your business venture, validating it in your mind and on your tax return. It acknowledges that you're not just dabbling; you're committed, you're professional, and your home office is a legitimate part of your business operation.

However, there's always the question of permanence. If your usage of an area as a home office fluctuates, or if you're moving desks and equipment in and out, you might struggle to establish the consistency the IRS looks for. Consult with a tax professional if your situation is fluid to ensure you're on solid ground.

In conclusion, your home office isn't just your business's command center; it's a tool in the tax savings toolkit. Armed with knowledge and thorough documentation, the home office deduction isn't merely a possibility—it's a strategy that can reduce your tax burden and reflect the pride you take in your entrepreneurial journey. Use it wisely!

Lest we forget, the home office deduction is just one piece of the puzzle. As we continue to navigate the twists and turns of tax deductions and credits, remember that each piece is a step towards a more profitable and sustainable business. So keep your records straight, know the rules, and claim what's rightfully yours to maintain momentum in this daring enterprise we call solo entrepreneurship.

Retirement Savings for Solo Entrepreneurs: Tax-Deferred Options

You've mastered the art of turning passions into profits, but have you untangled the intricacies of planning for retirement as a solo entrepreneur? We're talking about tax-deferred retirement savings that can significantly lower your taxable income now while securing your golden years. Crafting a comfortable retirement doesn't have to be a pipe dream, even without the cushion of a corporate 401(k) match. Solutions like SEP-IRAs, SIMPLE IRAs, and Solo 401(k) plans are designed specifically for the self-employed maverick, allowing you to stow away substantial amounts of income. These plans don't just offer future security; they come with tangible tax benefits today. With each contribution, you're not only building your nest egg but also reducing your current tax bill, creating a win-win scenario. By leveraging these solo entrepreneur-friendly retirement vehicles, you're laying the groundwork for a future that's just as vibrant and dynamic as your business life today. It's about harnessing the power of now to prepare for the what-ifs of later—because after all, your future self deserves the same level of care and dedication that you give to your clients.

SEP-IRA, SIMPLE IRA, and Solo 401(k) Plans As a solo entrepreneur, understanding the full spectrum of retirement options available to you is vital not just for your future financial stability but also for your current tax situation. These plans are power tools in your entrepreneurial toolkit, allowing you to save for retirement while reducing your taxable income. Let's dig into each of these options and unravel how they can significantly benefit your business and personal finances.

First up is the SEP-IRA, or Simplified Employee Pension Individual Retirement Account. This plan is a favorite among self-employed individuals due to its high contribution limits and straightforward administration. With a SEP-IRA, you can contribute up to 25% of your net earnings from self-employment, with a cap that adjusts for inflation each year. This elasticity in contribution limits can give you the flexibility to save more in good years and pull back during leaner times.

Moving on, let's not overlook the SIMPLE IRA, which stands for Savings Incentive Match Plan for Employees Individual Retirement Account. Slightly different from the SEP, the SIMPLE IRA is geared more toward small businesses with fewer than 100 employees, which often includes solo entrepreneurs. The real charm of the SIMPLE IRA lies in its simplicity—hence the name. You can set aside a portion of your income pre-tax, and if you have employees, you're required to contribute on their behalf either through a match or a fixed percentage.

Then there's the Solo 401(k), a heavyweight in the arena of solo retirement plans. Also called the individual 401(k), this plan mimics the traditional 401(k) plans offered by larger corporations but is designed specifically for self-employed individuals with no employees. What's unique about the Solo 401(k) is that it allows you to save as both the employer and the employee, thus enabling higher potential contributions. You can put away money as an employee of your business, and additionally, make employer non-elective contributions up to 25% of your compensation.

Choosing between these plans can seem daunting, but key factors to consider include the complexity of each plan's administration, your revenue, and whether you anticipate hiring employees in the future. For instance, if you're a high-earner looking to maximize your contributions, the SEP-IRA or Solo 401(k) might be the better choices due to their higher limits compared to the SIMPLE IRA.

Another essential aspect to weigh is the potential for loans and early withdrawals. A Solo 401(k) plan may allow you to borrow from your retirement savings, a feature that isn't available in SEP and SIMPLE IRAs. This could provide some peace of mind, knowing you have access to funds in case of an emergency—just remember that there are strict rules and potential tax consequences if you go down this route.

Tax planning with these retirement options can be incredibly advantageous. Contributions to SEP-IRA, SIMPLE IRA, and Solo 401(k) plans reduce your taxable income because they're made with pre-tax dollars. This lowers your tax bill in the year you make the contributions and can often place you in a lower tax bracket, yielding even more savings.

It's important to note the deadline for setting up and contributing to these accounts. Typically, SEP-IRA and Solo 401(k) plans must be established by the end of the fiscal year for which they will apply, although contributions can sometimes be made up until the tax-filing deadline, including extensions.

Furthermore, while the SEP-IRA and Solo 401(k) offer comparable contribution limits, the Solo 401(k) includes a catch-up contribution feature for participants 50 years of age and older, which is not available in the SEP-IRA. This feature can be incredibly valuable for those looking to accelerate their retirement savings later in their careers.

Don't forget to also consider the potential cost and administrative duties associated with each plan. SEP-IRAs generally have lower setup and maintenance costs than Solo 401(k) plans. However, the additional flexibility and loan feature of a Solo 401(k) may justify the extra cost and complexity for some business owners.

Each of these plans also has distinct paperwork requirements. For example, while the SEP-IRA is known for minimal paperwork, the Solo 401(k) may require an annual report to be filed with the IRS if your account exceeds certain thresholds. Ensuring timely and accurate paperwork will maintain the tax-favored status of your retirement plan and prevent unnecessary headaches.

While the SEP and SIMPLE IRAs are relatively quick to set up, establishing a Solo 401(k) can require more time and effort. However, the return on investment in terms of both potential tax savings and retirement preparation can make the Solo 401(k) an option worth exploring for many solo entrepreneurs.

Also, realize that you're not locked into one plan forever—you can change your plan if your business needs or retirement goals evolve. However, this often requires closing one account and opening another, which might incur additional taxes and penalties, so strategic planning is paramount.

Lastly, keep in mind the impact of your retirement plan choices on your future retirement income. While the immediate tax savings can be appealing, the ultimate goal is to ensure you have enough money to enjoy your retirement. Working with a financial planner can help you map out a retirement strategy that complements your tax planning and aligns with your long-term financial well-being.

To sum up, SEP-IRA, SIMPLE IRA, and Solo 401(k) plans are potent instruments for tax-saving and retirement planning for the solo entrepreneur. They can help you craft a financially secure future and offer flexibility in how you manage both your business and personal wealth. Reflect on your business needs, consult professionals when necessary, and make the right choices to maximize your benefits from these indispensable retirement vehicles.

Health Insurance and Medical Expenses: Navigating Deductions

For many solo entrepreneurs, the world of health insurance and medical expenses can be both confusing and costly. But did you know this perplexing area can also unlock significant tax deductions for the astute business owner? Let's explore how you can make the most of your medical-related expenses come tax time.

Firstly, if you're self-employed and paying for your own health insurance, you may be able to deduct 100% of your premium costs directly from your income. This is a personal deduction you take on your Form 1040 and isn't limited to your business expenses. Essentially, it can lower your adjusted gross income, which in turn can potentially drop you into a lower tax bracket, saving you money across the board.

Keep in mind, eligibility for this deduction is nuanced. For example, if you're eligible to participate in a spouse's employer-subsidized health plan, you might not qualify. Make sure to understand the specific stipulations to avoid a misstep here.

Aside from insurance premiums, other out-of-pocket medical expenses can also be tapped for deductions, although these are subject to specific thresholds. Generally, you can only deduct the amount of your total medical expenses that exceeds 7.5% of your adjusted gross income. This includes payments for diagnoses, treatments, as well as preventative measures, and could also encompass travel expenses related to medical care.

To take advantage of these deductions, meticulous record-keeping is paramount. This isn't just for compliance; it helps you understand your finances better, enabling you to make smarter decisions. So as you go through the year, keep hold of receipts for health insurance premiums, doctor's visits, laboratory fees, prescription drugs, and the like.

You may also be able to deduct long-term care insurance within certain limits. As an entrepreneur, preparing for every eventuality is part of your job description—ensuring that you're covered for long-term care without breaking the bank is just smart planning. Keep an eye on the federal limits for long-term care insurance deductions as these can change annually.

Let's not forget Health Savings Accounts (HSAs). Contributing to an HSA can give you a triple tax advantage: contributions are tax-deductible, the money grows tax-deferred, and withdrawals for qualified medical expenses are tax-free. As of this writing, you must be enrolled in a high-deductible health plan to qualify to use an HSA. It's a win-win-win situation if you're eligible.

Flexible Spending Arrangements (FSAs) are another consideration, although less common for sole proprietors, since you can't have an FSA and be the employer at the same time. However, if you have a separate business structure with employees, offering an FSA benefits both you and your team by reducing taxable income.

Dental and vision care are areas where people often overlook deductions. Dental insurance premiums and payments for services like cleaning, x-rays, or orthodontics can be included in your medical expense deductions. The same holds true for vision care—expenses for eye exams, glasses, contacts, and even corrective surgery are deductible.

For those with disabilities or chronic health issues, home modifications and special equipment can be deductible if they're medically necessary. This isn't just about ramps and lifts; it can include air filters, humidifiers, or alterations to cabinets and fixtures to make a home more accessible. Remember, these modifications must be a medical necessity, not just for general health and wellbeing.

When it comes to medical-related travel expenses, ensure you track every mile you drive to medical appointments, every bus fare, and even parking fees. These can add up and contribute to your threshold for deductions.

Now, with the dynamic nature of tax laws, make sure you're current on recent changes affecting health insurance and medical expense deductions. Legislation such as the Affordable Care Act can introduce new facets to consider, and often, modifications to deductions and limits happen yearly.

Lastly, it's critical to know when to seek help. Navigating deductions for health insurance and medical expenses can become complex, so consulting a tax professional with specific experience in this area is often a wise investment. They can assist in identifying all the deductions you're eligible for, ensuring you don't leave money on the table.

To conclude, managing health insurance and medical expenses is a challenge, but with the right approach, it's an area ripe with opportunities for tax deductions. By maintaining organized records, staying informed on the rules, and seeking assistance when necessary, you can significantly reduce your tax bill through these often-overlooked deductions. Remember, your health isn't just an expense—it's an investment, and managing it wisely can pay dividends both personally and financially.

Carry this attention to detail into every facet of your business, and you'll not only maintain your health but also the health of your enterprise. Thriving physically and financially is a balancing act, but with knowledge and a proactive attitude, you're setting yourself up for long-term success. In the next section, we'll delve into strategic tax planning, helping you further align your financial goals with savvy tax positioning.

Chapter 4:
Strategic Tax Planning for Solo Entrepreneurs

Transitioning from simply scrounging for every possible deduction, we now pivot to the methodical world of strategic tax planning. Every solo entrepreneur dreams of robust growth and financial stability, and, believe it or not, tax planning is your unsung partner in that journey. Mastering the art of timing can transform your tax situation, and it's as much about when you earn your income as it is about when you claim your expenses. As we delve into this chapter, you'll learn to navigate your tax bracket like a seasoned captain steering through unchartered waters, all while keeping an eye on the horizon for potential growth. It's about learning to dance with the tax codes—sliding in deductions here, deferring some income there—and making sure that every step you take builds towards a crescendo of optimal tax outcomes. It's not just about surviving year to year, but about crafting a tax approach that bolsters the foundation for your burgeoning enterprise. Armed with a compass of foresight, you can chart a course that not only handles today's liabilities but also shores up tomorrow's triumphs.

Understanding Your Tax Bracket and Planning for Future Growth

As we delve into the strategic tax planning realm for solo entrepreneurs, grasping the nuts and bolts of tax brackets becomes imperative. Your tax bracket isn't just a number— it's a window into your financial landscape, one that can influence everything from your pricing strategy to your investment decisions. Let's unravel the mystique around tax brackets and how knowledge of them can fuel not only your compliance but also your growth aspirations.

Firstly, tax brackets are a series of income ranges taxed at progressively higher rates. As a solo entrepreneur, you'll generally find yourself in a different tax bracket each year as your income fluctuates. It's like climbing a ladder; as you make more money, you ascend to higher rungs with corresponding higher rates. This is the essence of what we call a progressive tax system.

Knowing which bracket you're in isn't just trivia. It's about recognizing how much of your next dollar earned will go to taxes. If you're teetering on the edge of a higher tax bracket, it might influence your decision to accelerate or defer income— strategies we'll touch base on later.

Your bracket can also inform your retirement planning. Retirement accounts like traditional IRAs or Solo 401(k)s offer tax deductions on contributions, effectively lowering your taxable income today, with the tradeoff of paying taxes on withdrawals in retirement. If you're expecting to be in a lower bracket in retirement, saving through these accounts can mean paying less tax overall on your hard-earned money.

Planning for growth also involves understanding how additional income affects not only the tax on that income but potentially other fiscal aspects. Phases out of certain credits or deductions as your income climbs can sometimes be a stealthy tax increase that doesn't show up in the bracket percentage. It's crucial to anticipate these shifts and to plan accordingly.

One concept often overlooked by solo entrepreneurs is taxable efficiency. This means prioritizing income sources that are favored by tax rules. For example, long-term capital gains are taxed at lower rates than short-term gains. As you shift gears towards growth, aligning your investment strategies with tax efficiency could save you a significant amount in taxes over time.

While scaling up, the structure of your enterprise may swing the pendulum of tax efficiency. Many solo entrepreneurs start as sole proprietors, but as they grow, they might consider an LLC or electing S corporation status. Each structure has its implications on your taxes and tax bracket. An S corporation, for example, may allow you to split your income between salary and distributions, potentially lowering self-employment taxes.

Now, let's talk about tax planning beyond the present year, looking at multiple years to maximize tax benefits. This multi-year outlook involves projecting your future income and expenses to maneuver into favorable tax positions. It might include deferring income into a year where you expect to be in a lower bracket or accelerating expenses into a higher-income year to offset the tax impact.

Your business's life cycle stage is another cog in the wheel. Beginning stages often involve reinvestment and lower income, while maturity might bring stability and higher profits. Understanding this progression allows you to make informed decisions, like perhaps delaying a large purchase to a year where it can offset higher income.

Life events can also play a monumental role. Getting married, purchasing a home, or having children are just a few touchpoints that alter your tax landscape, hence involving them in your tax planning is critical. The addition of dependents or mortgage interest deductions could change your tax bracket and impact your business decisions.

Stay agile and ready to pivot when circumstances change. Taxes are just one part of your overall business strategy, but they can either support or hinder growth depending on how well they're managed.

Keep an eye on legislation changes, as they may present opportunities or require quick adaptation.

To sprout growth, harness the power of estimated tax payments. Making these payments quarterly helps manage your cash flow and avoids underpayment penalties. They force you to assess your income regularly, which loops back into staying on top of your tax bracket positioning.

Let's not forget, the aim is not just to save on taxes. Tax planning should be integrated with your overall financial goals. Yes, tax savings can fuel growth, but they should also reinforce the stability and long-term vision of your enterprise.

Endeavor to foster relationships with tax professionals who understand the unique landscape of solo entrepreneurship. A tax advisor can be a critical ally, guiding you through the shifting sands of tax brackets and planning strategies that align with your growth trajectory.

Finally, think of tax planning as an ongoing exercise, not just an annual event. Embed it into your monthly reviews, your investment decisions, your business structure considerations, and you'll find that managing your tax bracket is less of a scramble and more of a strategic maneuver towards a robust financial future.

In essence, understanding your tax bracket isn't about dodging taxes or toeing the line of legality — it's about empowering yourself to make decisions that nurture your business today and set the stage for tomorrow's success. It's an integral piece of the puzzle in the grand scheme of growing your solo enterprise.

Timing Income and Deductions for Optimal Tax Outcomes

Lean in close, because this is where the strategic planning ramps up and can truly enhance your fiscal fitness. As a solo entrepreneur, timing is more than just a buzzword—it's a powerful tool. Getting a grip on when to recognize income and when to take deductions can move the needle on your tax bill in a significant way. It's like a dance where you match your income with your deductions to the rhythm of the tax year. Consider accelerating expenses to offset a year that's been particularly profitable, or maybe you'll want to defer income as December 31 looms closer and it looks like you'll scale into a higher tax bracket. Juggling these decisions isn't just jargon; it's your hard-earned money staying where it belongs—in your pocket. Dive into the precision of perfect timing, and it's not just about working hard but working smart with every transaction. By mastering this strategy, you're setting the stage for some welcome tax savings that preserve the fruits of your labor for future growth or investment.

Year-End Tax Moves to Consider

As you approach the end of the fiscal year, it's the perfect time to reflect and make strategic tax moves that could lower your bill come April. Let's dive into some year-end strategies you might want to consider to optimize your finances and save on taxes.

Firstly, check if you've maximized contributions to your retirement accounts, such as your SEP-IRA, SIMPLE IRA, or Solo 401(k). Not only will this bolster your nest egg, but it also reduces your taxable income. Contributions can often be made up until the tax filing deadline but making them now can help you plan better for your tax outlay.

Next, consider the timing of your income and expenses. Can you delay invoicing for some of this year's work to push revenue into the next year, lowering this year's taxable income? Similarly, can you prepay expenses that you know you'll incur soon to claim those deductions now? This balancing act can be particularly impactful if you expect a change in your tax bracket.

On the topic of deductions, are there investments in equipment or technology that you've been putting off? Making those purchases before year-end can give you access to deductions, such as Section 179 or bonus depreciation, which can be a significant boon to your tax situation.

Don't overlook charitable contributions. Donating cash or property can not only be a fulfilling way to give back to the community but also offers tax deductions. Ensure you keep proper documentation for any donations you make.

Reviewing your health insurance plans and making use of a Health Savings Account (HSA), if you're eligible, can provide both health security and tax advantages. Contributions are tax-deductible, and funds grow tax-free for medical expenses.

Consider clearing your stocks portfolio of any underperformers. Selling securities at a loss can offset capital gains taxes you might have incurred from selling profitable investments earlier in the year.

If you've had a particularly good year, increasing your estimated tax payment could help you avoid underpayment penalties. Consult with your tax advisor to see if making a larger estimated tax payment before year's end is a smart move for you.

Small business owners also have the opportunity to set up a qualified retirement plan before the year's end if they don't already have one. This move could lead to significant tax savings both in the current and forthcoming years.

Look into whether you're eligible for any additional tax credits. Energy-efficient improvements to your home office, for instance, could qualify you for a residential energy credit, helping to cut down your tax liability.

Analyze your accounts receivable. If you have any bad debts from customers that you've been unable to collect, you may be able to write them off if you've previously included those amounts in your income.

Also, take stock of your current financial situation and see if a year-end bonus to yourself makes sense. If you're operating as an S corporation or a C corporation, paying out profits as a bonus can reduce business income, potentially lowering corporate tax rates.

If you plan to donate to charity and have appreciated stock, consider a charity stock donation. Donating stock directly to a charity, instead of selling it and then donating the cash, can help you avoid capital gains tax and still give you a charitable deduction for the full market value.

For those with kids or dependents, you might want to explore contributing to or setting up education savings plans, such as 529 plans. Although contributions to these plans are not deductible on your federal tax return, they could qualify for state tax deductions and grow tax-free for qualified education expenses.

And lastly, as we near the end of the current tax year, it's an excellent time to consult with a tax professional. Navigating the complexities of tax law and year-end strategies can be daunting, and personalized advice may uncover opportunities unique to your situation.

By considering these year-end tax moves, you're not just preparing for the upcoming tax season, you're actively shaping your financial future. It's about understanding the controllable factors in your taxation and taking measured steps to optimize where possible. Always stay proactive, and remember that your decisions now can affect your tax outcomes for years to come.

Chapter 5:
Sales Tax and Solo Entrepreneurs

As we transition from the strategic vantage point of tax planning into the more granular details of day-to-day fiscal responsibilities, it's crucial to spotlight one of the more nuanced yet impactful areas: sales tax. If you're selling goods or services, understanding when and how to administer sales tax is a fundamental aspect of staying compliant and avoiding legal pitfalls. Many solo entrepreneurs might find themselves inadvertently overlooking the maze of sales tax regulations, especially when dealing with customers across different states. Take heart in knowing that, while sales tax can seem daunting, it's a manageable element of your business operations with a bit of insight and organization. We'll guide you in distinguishing when sales tax should be on your radar and provide foundational steps to handle its collection without letting it overshadow the innovative spirit that fuels your solo venture. Stay vigilant yet undaunted; with precision and attention to detail, you can navigate sales tax waters skillfully, ensuring that these obligations don't deter you from your entrepreneurial journey.

When and How to Collect Sales Tax

After diving deep into the heart of income taxes, let's pivot to a subject just as crucial for the solo entrepreneur—sales tax. Because when it comes to sales tax, the mantra 'know before you owe' can save you bucket loads of stress and potential penalties down the line. Collecting sales tax isn't optional; it's a legal requirement that comes with the joy of selling goods and services, and understanding the 'when' and 'how' is non-negotiable.

To begin, the 'when' of collecting sales tax hinges on nexus. Nexus is a fancy term for a significant presence within a state. Once you've established nexus, you're playing in that state's sales tax sandbox. It's not just about your physical presence anymore; thanks to recent legal changes, even your digital footprint can trigger nexus.

How do you know if you've crossed the nexus threshold? The rules can be as diverse as the states themselves, and for the digital-savvy entrepreneurs among us, hitting a sales or transaction number in a specific state can ring the nexus bell. It's important to track not just where you are, but where your customers are, accounting for every digital breadcrumb leading back to your business.

Now, on to the 'how.' Life would be a walk in the park if there was a one-size-fits-all method for collecting sales tax, but that's not our reality. Each state has its own set of rates and rules. It's like fifty fiddly puzzles, and you've got to know which piece fits where. If you're selling physical products, the responsibility is on you to collect sales tax at the point of sale. It's straightforward—charge, collect, and then remit to the respective state government.

If your trade is in services, take a breath here, because that can be trickier. Not all services are taxed, and it varies wildly from state to state. Research is your best friend in this case. Ensure you're crystal clear on whether your services fall under taxable categories before billing your first client.

Now, we've got to talk about rates. Most areas have a base state rate, and then localities tack on additional percentages. There are tools aplenty online to help you calculate these rates precisely, because getting this wrong isn't just embarrassing—it could lead to shortchanging the tax authorities. And believe me, they will notice if you're not giving them their due slice of the pie.

For taxable sales online, consider your ecommerce platform as your partner in crime (legally, of course). Many platforms offer built-in sales tax collection services that align with your nexus obligations. These systems can be set up to add the correct tax based on the buyer's location, streamlining the process and leaving less room for error.

Don't forget about exemptions. Some customers—like resellers or non-profit organizations—may be exempt from sales tax. In this case, you'll need to obtain and keep valid exemption certificates. If the IRS comes knocking, you'll want to show them that everything is on the up and up.

Once the sales tax is collected, don't let it sit too long in your accounts. Every state has its filing schedule—monthly, quarterly, or annual. Mark your calendar, set reminders, do whatever it takes not to miss these deadlines. Late payments can incur penalties, and that's not a road you want to travel down.

Submitting sales tax returns could have been a chapter on its own. This isn't a one-click process; preparation is key. You'll often need to report sales for each jurisdiction where you collected tax. It's meticulous work, but every correctly filled line is a step away from potential audits.

Speaking of audits—keep your records sorted and accessible. In the rare case that you are audited, sales tax records will be gold. Store every invoice, exemption certificate, and return filed. Good recordkeeping isn't just about being organized; it's about protecting your business and your peace of mind.

For all this talk of responsibility and obligation, let's not forget technology's role in making your life easier. Sales tax software can automate almost every aspect of this process. It's not cheating; it's smart business. Investing in these tools is investing in accuracy and efficiency, and in turn, your own serenity.

What's vital to remember is that as your business grows, your sales tax responsibilities may expand. Keep a keen eye on your sales and their geographical spread. If you're about to hit or have hit threshold in new states, it's time to register for a sales tax permit in those jurisdictions. Yes, it's more work, but it's also a sign that your business is thriving—embrace the growth.

To put all this into perspective, remember that sales tax is not your money—it's the state's. You're just the middleman. By not treating sales tax with the respect it demands, you're putting your business at risk. It's not just about following the law; it's about safeguarding the integrity of your enterprise.

As we wrap up on sales tax, let's not be daunted by the complexity. Instead, let's approach it as we do every challenge in our solo journeys—with perseverance, intelligence, and a dash of creativity. Keep learning, stay organized, and use the tools at your disposal to ensure that when it comes to sales tax, you're always ahead of the game.

Now that you've got the gist of when and how to collect sales tax, the next section will navigate you through the labyrinth of multi-state sales tax compliance. Because, like it or not, tax is a dynamic landscape, and we must be adept navigators. So, keep your compass handy—we're steering through the multifaceted world of state taxes next!

Navigating Multi-State Sales Tax Compliance

The landscape of sales tax can be as varied and complex as the terrain of the United States itself, and for solo entrepreneurs selling across state lines, it's a domain that demands careful navigation. You've already mastered the basics of collecting sales tax within your home state, but what happens when your goods or services cross into other states? This is where multi-state sales tax compliance comes into play, an area where even the boldest of solo entrepreneurs must tread with caution to ensure that their venture remains on the right side of the law.

Contrary to what you might hope, there isn't a one-size-fits-all approach to handling sales tax in multiple states. Each state has its own set of rules, and as an entrepreneur, you're responsible for understanding and adhering to each where applicable. It all begins with the concept of 'nexus.' In the context of sales tax, nexus is the connection between a business and a state that requires the business to collect and remit sales tax in that state. It sounds straightforward, but it's the nuances that will catch you off guard if you're not meticulous.

The most common cause of nexus is physical presence. If you have a store, an office, or even a warehouse in a state, you likely have nexus there. But in today's digital age, the definition has stretched to include other activities, like attending trade shows, hiring remote employees, and even reaching a certain threshold of sales in a state. This expanded definition arose from the 2018 South Dakota v. Wayfair, Inc. Supreme Court ruling, which ushered in the era of 'economic nexus.'

Economic nexus pivots on your sales activity. If you surpass a state's sales revenue or transaction volume threshold, you create economic nexus, obligating you to collect and remit sales tax. It's critical you're aware of these thresholds, as they can vary widely by state. Some states have a threshold as low as $100,000 in sales or 200 transactions, while others have no economic nexus laws at all.

To keep your head above water in this complex regulatory environment, an organized approach to tracking your sales is indispensable. Maintain detailed records of where your customers are, how much they're spending, and how often they're buying. Ignorance isn't bliss in the realm of sales tax; it's a one-way ticket to non-compliance penalties. Knowledge is power, and in this case, it's also the foundation of your compliance strategy.

Once you've determined that you have nexus in one or more states, it's time to tackle registration. Each state requires you to register for a sales tax permit before you can legally collect sales tax. This process can usually be completed online through the state's department of revenue website. Don't overlook this step; collecting sales tax without a permit can lead to more severe consequences than not collecting it at all.

When it comes to actually collecting the sales tax, you'll face another layer of complexity—determining the right tax rate. States can have multiple tax rates based on the region, county, or city. Tools and software are available to help you calculate the correct rate, but you must stay vigilant as tax rates can change, and you need to apply the correct rate at the time of sale.

After collection, the next hurdle is the remittance of the sales tax. Each state will have its filing frequencies—monthly, quarterly, or annually—and deadlines. What's more, some states offer discounts for timely or early filings, which can be a nifty little perk for those entrepreneurs who like to stay ahead of the game.

Audit risk is also a stark reality that comes with multi-state sales tax compliance. States are increasingly savvy in their methods for tracking down non-compliant businesses, and they have much to gain by doing so. Audit exposure can be mitigated by maintaining scrupulous records, being proactive in your compliance efforts, and using automated systems to track and remit sales taxes. These tools not only take the grunt work out of the processes but also greatly reduce the risk of human error.

It's tempting to think of sales tax compliance as a static task, completed once and then forgotten. This couldn't be further from the truth. Laws change, business grows, and what worked for you last year might not cut it this year. Regularly reviewing your sales tax processes and staying up-to-date with legislative updates in each state where you have nexus is non-negotiable. If that sounds like a lot to handle, don't worry; once you've set up a solid system, staying informed is more about maintenance than overhaul.

Of course, the specter of non-compliance and its penalties looms large, and it's no wonder that this can be a source of anxiety for solo entrepreneurs. The consequences range from fines and penalties to, in severe cases, legal action. However, it's important to note that states often have voluntary disclosure programs allowing businesses to come into compliance with a clean slate. If you realize you've dropped the ball, don't hesitate to look into these programs. Acting quickly could save you from harsher penalties down the road.

We've talked about the stick, but let's not forget the carrot. There are reasons to smile when handling sales tax compliance across states. Being diligent in this area not only protects you from legal and financial pitfalls but can also engender trust in your business relationships. Your customers, partners, and suppliers can rest assured that you're a legitimate and law-abiding entrepreneur, which is always good for business.

Finally, if multi-state sales tax compliance is becoming a beast too burdensome for you to bear alone, remember that help is available. You're the entrepreneurial spirit; outsourcing tasks that don't require your unique touch isn't admitting defeat—it's smart business. Tax professionals and specialized software can transform a tangled web of tax obligations into a streamlined, manageable process, leaving you free to focus on what you do best—growing your business.

In conclusion, navigating multi-state sales tax compliance is no walk in the park, but with diligence, organization, and perhaps some professional assistance, it's far from impossible. Embrace it as part of the challenge and satisfaction of running your own business. Each tax permit obtained, each proper rate applied, each on-time filing—it's all evidence of your commitment to your entrepreneurial journey. And each step taken in compliance builds a firmer foundation for your business's longevity and success.

Chapter 6:
Dealing with Debt and Financial Challenges

After steering through the complex waters of sales tax, we now anchor in the troubled tides of debt and financial hurdles—a reality many solopreneurs face at some point. Let's dive into the nitty-gritty of handling debt without capsizing your business. Tax implications can arise from various sources of debt, especially when debt gets forgiven or restructured. Knowing the ins and outs of these tax rules is key to keeping your financial ship afloat. Moreover, maintaining a robust cash flow isn't just crucial for day-to-day business operations; it's also your lifeline to prevent the rough seas of tax penalties. Seasoned solo sea-captains and fresh sailors alike must chart a course for smooth financial sailing, even when the economic winds blow unfavorably. This chapter will not only throw you a lifeline but teach you how to swim adeptly through the choppy waters of business finance. By taming your cash flow and decoding the tax intricacies of debt, your solo venture can weather any stormy challenge ahead.

Tax Implications of Business Debt Forgiveness

As you navigate through the chapters of financial wisdom, tackling debt might stand out like an unavoidable pothole on the road to business success. Understandably, debt forgiveness might seem like a dream come true, lifting you out of financial quicksand. However, before you jump for joy, it's critical to zoom in on the tax implications that come with this relief. This is where the delicate dance of managing the benefits against potential tax liabilities begins.

Firstly, let's clarify what we mean by debt forgiveness. It occurs when a lender decides not to hold you responsible for paying back a portion, or even the entirety, of your debt. Sounds like a financial lifeline, doesn't it? But it's not without strings attached, as the IRS often views the forgiven amount as taxable income. As a savvy entrepreneur, you'll want to grasp the nuances of this tax treatment, so you don't end up swapping one financial burden for another.

The crux of the matter lies with the IRS's infamous Form 1099-C, "Cancellation of Debt." When your lender forgives or cancels a debt greater than $600, you can expect to receive this form. It's a signal to roll up your sleeves and ready yourself for some additional tax math. The amount of the forgiven debt is generally reported on your tax return as "other income," and yes, this could inflate your taxable income for the year, leading to a potentially higher tax bill.

However, don't let your heart rate spike just yet. The tax code provides exceptions and exclusions that could dramatically alter your situation. If you're insolvent — meaning your total liabilities exceed the fair market value of your total assets — right before the debt is forgiven, you might not have to report your forgiven debt as income. Documenting your financial status at the time of forgiveness is key, so you'll want to keep meticulous records.

Another escape route lies with bankruptcy. If the debt was discharged through a bankruptcy proceeding, you don't usually have to include the forgiven amount in your income. But tarry not, for careful documentation and professional advice are essential in navigating these legal and financial waters.

Now, if your forgiven debt was tied to a loan on property, things get a bit more complex with nuances like "recourse" and "nonrecourse" debts. With recourse debts, you could be on the hook for taxable income based on the difference between the outstanding loan and the fair market value of the property. Nonrecourse debts get a bit of a pass since their nature means the lender can't pursue you beyond the collateral value.

Small business owners who operate as sole proprietors, or in some cases, partnerships and S corporations, may also find relief under the Qualified Real Property Business Indebtedness exclusion. This little gem of the tax code allows you to exclude forgiven debt from your income if it was used to acquire or improve property used in your business. But heed this: the exclusion will require you to reduce certain tax attributes, which can affect future deductions.

For the farming community among entrepreneurs, the Qualified Farm Indebtedness exclusion can be a beacon of hope. Similar to the aforementioned exclusion, it lets you leave off certain canceled debts from your income report, provided your loan was directly associated with the operation. But don't gallop off just yet; the specifics of farm indebtedness are as intricate as they are vital, so attention to detail is paramount.

Now, don't get blindsided by the possibility of a tax bill following debt forgiveness. An ounce of prevention is worth a pound of cure — setting aside funds in anticipation of the tax liability can alleviate the stress. It's all about planning, and as a business owner, you know that foreseeing challenges and preparing for them is half the battle.

Should you find yourself in the land of debt forgiveness, a proactive step is to seek consultation with a tax professional. Tax laws and regulations can be as fickle as the wind, frequently changing trajectories. Ensuring you have the most current and tailored advice will set you up to navigate these scenarios with less trepidation.

One strategy that might be tempting is to try and work out a deal with your creditor to report a smaller amount of forgiven debt. Caution should be your watchword here, as any discrepancy between what the creditor reports and what you file can unfurl a red flag, triggering unwanted attention from the IRS. Transparency and accuracy are your best allies in this financial minefield.

Lastly, we must consider how state tax laws interact with federal tax regulations. Some states may not conform to the federal tax treatment of canceled debts, which means you could be looking at a different set of rules when filing your state taxes. Always consider this additional layer when addressing the consequences of debt forgiveness.

The financial vitality of a solo venture can often hinge on the nuances of tax obligations. Debt forgiveness, while seemingly a stroke of luck, carries its own set of rules that must be navigated with a sturdy rudder. As you sail these waters, knowledge is power. A firm understanding of the tax implications will serve as a beacon, guiding you safely to the shores of financial stability and compliance.

Remember, as you roll with the punches that entrepreneurship throws your way, addressing tax implications head-on, with resolve and smarts, isn't just about riding out the storm — it's about emerging from it in a stronger position. With that in mind, let your next moves be deliberate and informed, with an aim towards not just surviving, but thriving in the face of financial challenges.

Managing Cash Flow to Avoid Tax Penalties

Keeping a steady hand on the tiller of your financial ship is essential, especially when it comes to navigating the turbulent waters of taxes. An intrinsic connection exists between cash flow management and tax obligations. One supports the other, and if your handling of cash flow is misaligned, tax penalties can quickly become a reality. Let's get to grips with balancing the two, ensuring that the taxman's share doesn't capsize your financial vessel.

A core aspect of managing your cash flow is being acutely aware of your tax payment schedules. The IRS isn't the most forgiving of creditors; they expect their dues on time. For the independent go-getters among us, quarterly estimated taxes can very much feel like a double-edged sword. On one hand, it's a display of independence and control over your financial obligations. On the other, missing these dates by even a day can lead to unnecessary and, quite frankly, avoidable penalties.

In managing your finances to avoid these penalties, being proactive is key. This doesn't just mean setting reminders before tax deadlines (although don't underestimate the power of a well-timed notification). It involves a more in-depth strategy where you align your cash inflows with your outflows. A strong understanding of your business cycle will help forecast when you'll have the most cash on hand to make those tax payments without feeling the pinch.

Budgeting for your tax liabilities isn't about setting aside a lump of cash and hoping it covers it. It's a fine-tuned process. Allocate a specific percentage of your income to a separate account designated for taxes, every time you get paid. This not only simplifies your tax payments but also prevents the temptation to dip into these funds for everyday expenses.

Now, let's talk about cash reserves. Building a reserve can be a lifesaver when unexpected expenses crop up or when a client payment is delayed. It also provides a buffer for tax payments on leaner months. The goal is to gather enough in your reserve to cover at least one quarter's worth of taxes. That way, you're not caught off-guard with bare coffers come tax time.

Another tip is to align your billing cycle with your tax cycle. If your business allows for it, schedule your invoices so that payments come in right before taxes are due. This ensures that you're not left scrambling for funds when the quarterly estimated taxes come knocking.

Of course, you can't manage what you don't understand. Diving deep into the IRS publications on self-employment and estimated taxes is a non-negotiable. They contain relevant details about when to pay, how much to pay, and the methods of payment acceptable to the IRS. Knowledge is power, and in this case, it could save you from financial stress.

Cash flow forecasting is an invaluable skill to master. By predicting your future cash position based on historical data, you can make informed decisions about how to use your funds. Forecasting helps you to adjust spending, delay non-essential purchases, or seek short-term financing options in advance of a dry spell.

Speaking of financing, always consider the implications of debt on your cash flow and tax situation. Loans are not inherently bad; they can offer a lifeline when needed. However, they must be managed judiciously. Calculate the cost of borrowing against your future cash projections to ensure you can service any debt and meet tax obligations simultaneously.

For many solo entrepreneurs, leveraging technology can be a game-changer for managing tax-related cash flow issues. A plethora of apps and software tools exist that can simplify budgeting, forecasting, and setting aside tax funds. More than just bells and whistles, these technologies provide actionable insights and reminders to keep you on financial track.

It's also wise not to go at it alone. A financial advisor or tax consultant can become your ally. They can help tailor a tax payment plan that matches your specific business needs and cash flow patterns. Sometimes, the cost of professional advice is far outweighed by the benefits and savings from avoiding penalties and optimizing tax liabilities.

Another critical component of managing cash flow is timely reconciling and bookkeeping. Regularly updating your financial records ensures you have a clear and current picture of your business finances. You can't afford to be in the dark about where you stand financially when tax deadlines approach.

Managing cash flow to avoid tax penalties is an ongoing process that evolves with your business. It takes discipline, foresight, and a proactive approach to financial management. But trust in the process – your solo operation has the potential to run as efficiently as any larger enterprise, with the added bonus of being nimble and adaptable.

To smooth out the ebb and flow of business income, consider diversifying your income streams. Having multiple sources of income can mitigate the impact of a client falling through or a project being delayed. Diversification doesn't just bolster your defense against the unpredictable; it steadies your cash flow, enabling you to cover those inevitable tax payments more comfortably.

Lastly, when dealing with tax penalties that have already occurred, don't let them fester. Address them immediately with the IRS, as options for payment plans or even penalty abatement do exist. Ignoring these issues will not make them vanish, and quick action can stop the penalties from compounding.

The cyclical relationship between cash flow management and meeting tax obligations is one that when respected, can reinforce the financial stability of your solo endeavor. It allows you to focus on growth and success, secure in the knowledge that your tax penalties are not just an avoided disaster, but an impossibility in your well-oiled machine. Lay a solid foundation in cash flow management, and the rest of your financial narrative will undoubtedly follow suit.

Chapter 7:
Tax Tips for Specific Solo Professions

As we turn the page from grappling with debt and financial turbulence, let's zoom in on the tax tips that cater to the unique needs of particular solo professions. No two paths are identical in the world of solitary hustles, and your tax strategy must reflect that singularity. If you're a freelance writer or an artist, there are industry-specific deductions that are just ripe for the picking, but you've got to know where to look. Consulting and coaching gurus, splitting your personal and business expenses can get tricky, but fear not, as a clear understanding of what constitutes as a legitimate business expense will pave the way. Real estate mavens, with your unique tax considerations, a deep dive into the nuances of property investments, depreciation, and your status as a real estate professional can unlock fresh savings. Each profession has its tax quirks and perks; we'll dissect them with precision, ensuring you exploit every avenue available to keep your hard-earned cash where it belongs—with you and your burgeoning solo enterprise.

Freelance Writers and Artists: Industry-Specific Deductions

For freelance writers and artists, mastering the canvas of tax deductions is as essential as honing their craft. Unlike more conventional jobs, these creatives have the ability to outline a tax narrative woven with a tapestry of unique deductions. Each brushstroke across the ledger can lead to significant savings, transforming the mundane task of taxes into an art form of financial prudence.

Let's commence with the studio, often your own home. A portion of your domestic space may qualify for the *home office deduction* if it's exclusively used for your business. Analyze the square footage dedicated to your work and you'll potentially delineate a deduction for rent, utilities, insurance, and even repairs, proportional to your office space. Remember, though, this space must be a principal place for conducting your business to qualify, so it's more than just a corner where inspiration strikes—it's your business hub.

Materials and supplies are the palette from which your art emerges. Canvas, ink, software subscriptions, research materials, or any other consumables necessary to produce your work are deductible. The key is to ensure they're ordinary and necessary for your craft—not extravagant, but essential to your day-to-day creation process.

Perhaps less glamorous but just as critical are costs related to *equipment and technology*. The computer that harbors your manuscripts, the camera capturing your visual narratives, or the printer that births hard copies—all can be depreciated or expensed using Section 179 or bonus depreciation. Don't ignore minor gadgets either; they can add up to sizable deductions.

Amidst the solitary hours, networking becomes a beacon. Membership dues for writers' guilds or artists' collectives and fees for attending conferences serve not only to enrich your skills but are also tax-deductible. However, draw a clear line—these events and organizations should be related to your profession to qualify.

Marketing your work—through websites, business cards, portfolio materials, and online ads—can be another well of deductible expenses. It's all about promoting your brand and selling your services. Just ensure the promotional activity is aligned with the aim of druming up business and not merely a vanity project.

Travel expenses can paint a pretty picture on your tax return if they're for business. A trip to a writers' conference, an art show, or a freelance gig miles away can include transportation, accommodation, and even a portion of your meals. But be scrupulous—it's critical to document the purpose and ensure it revolves around business, not leisure.

Educational expenses can be deductible when they maintain or improve your professional skills. Whether it's a writing workshop, art class, or an online course enhancing your techniques, these investments in your professional development are not merely enriching—they're often deductible.

Then there's the often overlooked but invaluable *self-employed health insurance deduction*. If you maintain your own health insurance, the premiums may be deductible—a substantial boon to the solopreneur protecting their health while nurturing their business.

Don't forget about subscription services and publications relevant to your trade. From literary journals to design magazines, these resources keep you current and can reduce your taxable income. Ensure these subscriptions directly benefit your work and aren't just casual reading.

The home internet and phone bill quickly morph from personal utilities to essential business tools for freelance writers and artists. A portion reflecting business use becomes eligible for deduction—streamlining your outreach and research without ignoring cost efficiencies.

What about agent or gallery fees? If you employ a representative to sell your writings or art, their commission is a line item that lowers your income. Agents and gallery spaces often take a sizeable cut but remember, this outlay represents a legitimate business expense.

Professional development comes in many shapes, but critiques and editorial services are particularly noteworthy for writers. While they might sting your ego, they nurture your career—and they're deductible. Quality critique or editing can elevate a piece from passable to professional, making this a wise investment for your business and tax situation.

Lastly, remember the humble but mighty business insurance—a safeguard against the unpredictable, its premiums are deductibles that promise security and peace of mind.

Wary of the intricacies? Fear not. Each meticulous record you keep is a defense against the plight of audits and ensures the accuracy of your deductions. As you navigate this labyrinth of potential savings, meticulous documentation is your guiding star.

In the grand tapestry of taxes for freelance writers and artists, these industry-specific deductions are threads that can be woven into a shelter against financial storms. Approach your tax duties with the creativity you apply to your work, and watch as the portrait of an optimized tax scenario is revealed. The genius of artistry isn't just found in creation—it's reflected in the strategic management of your fiscal responsibilities as well.

Consultants and Coaches: Splitting Personal and Business Expenses

Within the dynamic world of consulting and coaching, the line between personal and business expenses can often become blurred. As a savvy solo entrepreneur in this field, maximizing your tax savings relies on effectively categorizing these expenses. The key is to maintain crystal clarity about which of your expenditures serve your business and which ones cater to your personal life.

First things first: understanding the importance of an organized system to track expenses cannot be understated. Whether it's software or a simple spreadsheet, your system should be as meticulous as your consulting or coaching plans. This method will save you from headaches and maximize your deductions come tax time. It also stands as your first line of defense if the IRS comes knocking for an audit.

Business expenses for consultants and coaches usually include the direct costs of running your enterprise—the so-called 'necessary and ordinary' expenses like advertising, client workshops, and training materials. But what about that new laptop? If you use it exclusively for coaching sessions, client communication, and writing proposals, it's a business expense. If your kids use it for homework or you're binge-watching your favorite series, you've just tread into personal territory.

Home office deductions are a boon for consultants and coaches, but they're also a major red flag if not handled properly. If you have a space dedicated solely to your business, you're in the clear. The proportion of your home's expenses that correlate to your home office—like mortgage interest, rent, utilities, and insurance—can typically be deducted. Just make sure the space isn't doubling as a guest room on the weekends.

Another area to consider is travel. Networking events, conferences, client meetings—these are often necessary when building a successful consultancy or coaching business. Keep a detailed log of your travel expenses, including mileage records if you're driving. Remember, that trip to Hawaii only counts if there's a bona fide business purpose behind it, like attending a conference, not if you're squeezing in two hours of work by the poolside.

Now, for the delicate subject of meals and entertainment. Yes, discussing a client's business over dinner does qualify as a business expense. However, the IRS has tightened rules around these deductions, so make sure these expenses are reasonable and necessary. Extravagant meals won't fly unless you can substantiate their business purpose with clear documentation.

Telecommunication expenses can get particularly thorny. Your cellphone and internet service are essential tools, but only the percentage used for business can be written off. If you're fielding personal calls on the same phone, you need to prorate the expense. Software that helps you keep client appointments or manage your newsletter list? Those are fully deductible.

What about professional development? If you're upskilling through a coaching certification to enhance your business services, those expenses are generally deductible. But if the training is for personal interest or outside the scope of your current business, you can't include it. Keeping up with the latest in your field is not just smart—it's deductible.

Equipment and office supplies pose less of a gray area as long as they're used strictly for business. Yes to the ergonomic office chair that saves your back during long sessions of client calls, no to the PlayStation 5 that helps you unwind after. Striking the right balance is crucial here.

Personal development books and self-help materials can be another tricky area. Are they for personal fulfillment or professional consultation? If you can link them directly to improving your professional services, you can likely count them as a business expense. The lines can be fuzzy, so jot down notes on how each book relates to your business when making the purchase.

For insurance, if you have a policy that covers both your home and home office, or your vehicle for both business and personal use, it's important to split these costs appropriately. The portion of your insurance that protects your business assets is deductible. Always keep solid records to back up your claims.

When it comes to professional subscriptions, memberships, and software, as long as they benefit your business operations or enhance your knowledge in your consulting or coaching field, they are typically deductible. Be judicial and ensure these subscriptions directly correlate to the work you do.

Let's touch on gifts too. If you're sending a token of appreciation to a client, make sure it's modest. The IRS generally caps the deduction for business gifts at $25 per recipient per year. So, while a classy pen might be okay, a luxury watch will be largely out-of-pocket.

And finally, health insurance—a vital consideration for all solo entrepreneurs. Premiums for yourself, your spouse, and your dependents can often be deductible, provided your business is turning a profit. This one's a major benefit for solo consultants and coaches, so don't let it go unnoticed.

As we wrap up this chapter, remember, consulting and coaching are professions where personal and business lives may intertwine intimately. Understanding the rules and keeping diligent records is the name of the game. Approach your expense tracking with the same passion and precision you bring to your clients, and you'll navigate the tax labyrinth like a seasoned pro, reaping the rewards of well-managed finances and staying on the sunny side of tax compliance.

Real Estate Professionals: Unique Tax Considerations

Navigating the tax landscape as a real estate professional means more than just recording your mileage between property showings. Your financial canvas is extensive, covering everything from commissions and marketing expenses to travel costs and home office deductions. Getting a firm grip on these unique tax considerations not only enhances financial gains but ensures you stay in good graces with tax laws.

First, it's critical to understand the importance of your status as a 'real estate professional' for tax purposes. This isn't just a title—it's a designation that the IRS acknowledges and scrutinizes. Meeting the criteria involves substantial participation in real estate activities, which goes beyond dabbling in the occasional rental property. If you're spending considerable time managing, developing, or flipping properties, you need to demonstrate that real estate is your full-time gig to potentially benefit from associated tax breaks.

For starters, think about your workspace. Whether it's a Hi-Rise corner office or the cozy nook in your living room, real estate professionals often qualify for the *home office deduction*. Here's the catch—your space must be used regularly and exclusively for business. So, if you're also using your home office as a part-time yoga studio or your personal Netflix binge spot, you might need to reconsider claiming this deduction.

Moving through your expenses, let's chat about vehicle use. Driving to open houses, client meetings, or scouting new listings racks up miles, and those miles translate to deductions. Keep a detailed log of your travel for work—there's an array of apps designed for this—so you can accurately calculate the sizable deduction at year's end. Both the standard mileage rate and actual expense methods are available, but the key here is consistent and meticulous record keeping.

Don't overlook the swath of other deductibles—advertising, marketing materials, staging costs, professional association dues, and even certain educational expenses to stay current in your field. Every brochure, business card, and bill for a seminar or real estate class potentially slices a bit off your taxable income.

Acquiring property requires substantial outlay and here's where the concept of *depreciation* comes into play. As a real estate pro, you can depreciate the cost of buildings, not the land, over a set period, generally 27.5 years for residential and 39 years for commercial properties. It's a way of simulating the property's decreasing value over time, even if the market value is appreciating.

For those delving into rental properties, the *passive activity loss rules* are particularly relevant. Typically, losses from passive activities are only deductible against passive income, but as a real estate professional who materially participates in rental activities, you might elude this restriction, enabling you to apply rental losses against non-passive income. This is complex terrain, however, so here's where aligning with a tax expert could be invaluable.

Circling back to the 'real estate professional' status—it plays a huge role in how your rental income and losses are treated. If you pass the time and participation tests set forth by the IRS, you can avoid the passive activity loss limits, which can be particularly advantageous. Keep close tabs on the hours you clock in all of your real estate endeavors and be prepared to substantiate your involvement if challenged.

When you do nail that big commission, remember to set aside a portion for taxes. Real estate agents are not generally subject to withholding by employers, which means you're responsible for making estimated tax payments each quarter. Avoiding that end-of-year tax sting requires foresight and proactive financial planning.

Also, don't miss the boat on maximizing your retirement savings. As a self-employed individual, options like the SEP-IRA or Solo 401(k) present opportunities to tuck away a substantial sum for the golden years while simultaneously lowering your taxable income. There are limits and rules to follow, but the tax benefits are worth the strategic effort.

Understanding the tax implications of property sales is vital, too. Capital gains taxes loom over the horizon of any profitable sale. If you've held a property for more than a year, those gains are typically taxed at a lower rate than short-term ones. However, if you're flipping properties frequently, your gains could well be considered ordinary income, taxed at higher rates.

Weaving through the labyrinth of 1031 exchanges might also save you significant money. This strategy allows real estate investors to defer capital gains taxes by reinvesting proceeds from the sale of one property into the purchase of another. It's a powerful tool, but it's fitted with a tight set of rules to qualify. Again, this is not a do-it-yourself territory; professional guidance can prove to be a sound investment.

For the savvy real estate entrepreneur, there's also potential to tap into opportunity zone investments. These relatively new additions to the tax code offer deferred and potentially reduced capital gains for investments made in economically distressed communities. They require a long-term commitment but can be a noble and lucrative component of your tax strategy.

Lastly, remember to stay up-to-date with tax law changes—like the occasional adjust in mileage rates or shifts in how depreciation is approached. The ground in the realm of taxes is seldom still, especially in the dynamic world of real estate. Knowledge is power, and staying informed is the best way to leverage your tax position.

So there you have it—real estate is a unique beast in the tax world. Treat it with the respect and attention it demands, and your tax burden could feel much lighter. Look at each property, each transaction, each mile driven as a cog in the intricate machine of your tax strategy. It's this kind of careful consideration and planning that will smooth out the financial hills and valleys synonymous with the terrain of a real estate professional's career. Dive in, dig deep, and with shrewd tax maneuvering, your financial outlook can be just as striking as that perfectly staged home ready for sale.

Chapter 8:
Audits and Red Flags:
Staying on the Right Side of the IRS

So, you've navigated the choppy waters of setting up shop, meticulous record-keeping, and savvy tax planning—it's smooth sailing from here, right? Not so fast. Let's dive into one of the less-discussed, yet critically important aspects of tax management: avoiding audits and understanding the red flags that can attract unwanted attention from the IRS. While the thought of an audit may send shivers down your spine, the key is to remain calm and collected. Remember, staying compliant isn't rocket science—it's a matter of keeping your ducks in a row and understanding what might set off the IRS's radar. From overstated deductions to inconsistent reporting, some tripwires are more common than others. But fear not, by empowering yourself with the knowledge of what flags a return and how to prepare for any scrutiny that may come your way, you can maintain a confident stand and keep your business's integrity intact. Sailing close to the wind may work for some, but when it comes to taxes, you'll want to keep your vessel on the straight and narrow.

Common Audit Triggers for Solo Entrepreneurs

As we navigate through the labyrinth of tax rules and regulations prevalent for solo entrepreneurs, it's essential to stay abreast of the potential pitfalls that could lead you into the dreaded audit territory.

An audit doesn't necessarily mean you've done something wrong, but it does mean the IRS is double-checking to make sure your finances add up. Knowing what triggers an IRS audit can help keep your business clear of unwanted scrutiny.

One primary red flag is the misuse of the home office deduction. Solo entrepreneurs often take advantage of this deduction, but it's also frequently misrepresented. The IRS is clear on the criteria needed to qualify: the space must be regularly and exclusively used for business. It's tempting to fudge these rules, but let's not play with fire – ensure you're within guidelines to maintain peace of mind.

Another trigger could be reporting a higher than average amount of business expenses compared to your income. Excessive deductions can capture the IRS's attention. It's critical to only claim legitimate business expenses and maintain meticulous records to substantiate your claims. Large, round numbers on your tax return can also arouse suspicion – they suggest estimations rather than precise calculations.

Mixed use of business and personal expenses is a frequent issue for solo entrepreneurs. Getting too casual with using your business account for personal expenses, or vice versa, can lead to a blurry line that the IRS might want to clarify. Always maintain separate accounts and document each transaction's purpose rigorously.

Fluctuating income can also wave a red flag. Therapy for your fledgling business? Normal. But to the IRS, it may suggest something is awry. If your income drops dramatically or spikes suddenly, it may prompt the IRS to get curious about the cause. Always be prepared to explain large discrepancies from one year to the next.

Non-filing or late filing of tax returns is an obvious but still common trigger. Meeting tax deadlines is fundamental for staying off the IRS's radar. If you can't file or pay on time, don't go silent – communicate with the IRS and arrange an extension or payment plan.

Claiming 100% business use of a vehicle is another misstep that catches the IRS's eye. If you use a car for both business and personal transport, you'll need to allocate the usage accurately – and keep a detailed log to support your claims.

Cash businesses are inherently tricky when it comes to accurately reporting income. Because there's often a lack of electronic trails, they're on the IRS's watch list. Ensure that every penny is accounted for. Yes, it may be tedious, but it's infinitely preferable to an audit.

Math errors may seem minor but can trigger an audit if they're significant enough. Double and triple-check all calculations on your return. In the digital age, using tax software can mitigate this risk, as long as you input the correct information.

Lastly, a major trigger is not reporting all taxable income. This seems like a no-brainer, but discrepancies between your reported income and the information the IRS has from 1099s and other sources will most certainly raise some eyebrows. Every gig, every side hustle, every bit must be reported.

Audits are not inherently disastrous, but they can be stressful, time-consuming, and costly if they result in additional taxes owed with penalties and interest. Preventing audits before they happen is key. And here's the uplifting part – as a solo entrepreneur, you wield immense control over your financial and tax destiny. Use this power wisely, record meticulously, report accurately, and you're well on your way to steering clear of audit landmines.

One last piece of advice – if you've historically played fast and loose with these issues, it's never too late to course-correct. Begin this tax year with a new commitment to meticulousness and clarity in your tax matters. Your future self, the one without an IRS audit hanging over their head, will undoubtedly thank you.

All in all, the mantra to hold dear is simple: be transparent, be thorough, and maintain an organized trail of your business finances. With a steadfast approach to your tax obligations, you're fortifying yourself against potential audit risks. Ready to unleash the full potential of your solo journey with confidence and the wisdom to sidestep the common missteps? Let's move forward, attentive to these triggers, and keep our eyes on the prize: a thriving business in harmonious balance with tax compliance.

Preparing for and Handling an IRS Audit

When the IRS comes knocking, fear can be the first response, especially if you're a solo entrepreneur managing every aspect of your business. But take a breath—proper preparation and a calm approach can transform an audit into a manageable process. Let's unlock the mystique behind IRS audits and arm you with knowledge and strategies to handle them with confidence.

The key to a smooth audit experience lies in understanding what might trigger it. Common red flags include disproportionate deductions, frequent cash transactions, or significant changes in income. But remember, not all audits stem from suspicions; some are just a roll of the dice in the grand scheme of the IRS's random selection process.

Now, timing is everything. You'll typically be notified of an audit via letter, which will detail what aspects of your tax return are under review. Quick and thorough responsiveness can set the tone for efficient communication. Keep a copy of every correspondence with the IRS—trust me, you'll want a trail to follow should questions arise down the line.

Organization is your best defense against the storm of an audit. Hopefully, you've been keep meticulous records of income, expenses, and deductions, as instructed in previous chapters. It's essential to have them readily available and organized. If there are gaps, start filling them as soon as you can—legally and ethically, of course.

Understanding the specifics of what the IRS is examining will sharpen your focus. Is it your mileage logs, charitable contributions, or your home office deductions? Zero in on these areas and review the documentation standards the IRS expects. This attention to detail can often defuse potential issues before they ignite.

Many solo entrepreneurs worry about the cost of representation in an audit. Nonetheless, securing a knowledgeable tax advisor or CPA can be an invaluable investment. These professionals speak the language of the IRS and can often clear up misunderstandings that you may not be able to articulate as effectively.

Should you face an in-person audit, it's crucial to handle the interaction with professionalism. Be polite, stick to the facts and avoid offering unsolicited information. Let the documents speak for themselves and only elaborate when necessary. This isn't the time for personal stories; it's an examination of the numbers.

If the auditor brings up discrepancies, don't panic. Dig into your records and find the evidence that supports your filing. Sometimes a simple explanation is all that's needed to clarify confusion. If mistakes were made, be prepared to discuss how they happened; honesty is always the best policy.

Don't overlook the option of appealing the auditor's findings if you disagree. The IRS Office of Appeals is an independent body within the IRS that offers a fair platform to contest audit decisions without going to court. Knowing this can give you peace of mind that there are additional steps if needed.

During the audit process, maintain your routine business operations as usual. While dealing with an audit can be time-consuming, your ongoing business success shouldn't be sacrificed. Keep earning, keep recording, and keep planning for the future.

Income and deductions should continue being recorded with precision. If the IRS sees that you're steadfast in your practices, it not only helps your current audit situation but also fortifies your credibility for potential future interactions with the tax authorities.

One of the most empowering measures is to educate yourself on tax matters. Being informed softens the edges of the daunting prospect of an IRS audit. Read up on your rights, understand the possible outcomes, and know the timelines involved. Knowledge exudes confidence, and confidence is a strong ally.

Throughout the audit process, stay grounded and keep an eye on your emotional well-being. It can be stressful, but remember, an audit is not an accusation. It's a review, and like any review, it can have positive outcomes, like affirming your due diligence or highlighting where you can improve taxation practices.

Finally, learn from the experience. Whether the outcome is good or bad, there's always a lesson to be derived. Perfect your record-keeping, adjust your approach to deductions, or even revamp your accounting system. Each IRS audit can be a stepping stone to better tax health and a more robust business model.

Handling an IRS audit isn't merely about surviving the ordeal but emerging more robust and savvy on the other side. You're building a resilient business that can weather any storm, including the keen eyes of the IRS. Use the audit to reinforce your financial structure and forge ahead with the confidence of an entrepreneur who's fully in command of their tax journey.

Chapter 9:
Navigating Changes in Tax Law

As we pivot from the essential defense against audits in Chapter 8, it's time to master the art of staying agile when tax laws shift beneath our feet. Tax codes are as dynamic as the weather, constantly evolving with new legislation that can catch you off guard if you're not vigilant. As a solo entrepreneur, you can't afford to be left in the dust; understanding and adapting to these changes is crucial to safeguarding your hard-earned dough and staying compliant. Consider the tax landscape a game board where rules can change mid-play, impacting your strategy. It's essential to have a reliable information stream that keeps you abreast of the latest tax code updates. Embrace the challenge - with each new twist in tax laws, there's an opportunity to reassess and refine your approach, ensuring your tax strategy remains robust and responsive. Remember, when the winds of tax law change, it's your sails, not the gales, that determines the direction you go. Stay informed, be adaptable, and navigate these waters with confidence to turn new tax rules into fresh opportunities for financial success.

Staying Informed on Tax Law Updates

Tax laws are as dynamic as the economy itself, adapting to changes in societal priorities, fiscal needs, and political landscapes. As a solo entrepreneur, keeping abreast of these changes is not just about compliance; it's about seizing opportunities to optimize your tax position and safeguarding the financial health of your business. Just as you wouldn't navigate a ship without a compass, you shouldn't navigate tax season without staying updated on the latest tax law changes.

Start by setting a consistent schedule to check for updates. Tax authorities often release bulletins or newsletters that can be a primary source of information. Subscribing to these updates can provide you with real-time alerts on new laws, filing practices, and potential benefits you could be missing out on. Remember, forewarned is forearmed, and in tax planning, that translates to extra savings or avoided penalties.

Invest time in reading and understanding the implications of new tax laws. It's not enough to know that a law has changed, but grasp how it affects your bottom line. Some changes may call for alterations to your business structure, adjustments to your estimated tax payments, or revisions to your retirement contributions. The devil is in the details, and tax law is no exception. It's vital to your business that you understand not only what's changed, but how it specifically impacts you.

Make technology your ally in staying informed. There is a plethora of apps and online tools designed for tax planning and preparation that update automatically with the latest tax rules. These tools can help you apply new laws to your business scenario instantly without having to decipher complex tax jargon.

Don't overlook the value of tax professionals. A savvy accountant or tax advisor who specializes in working with solo entrepreneurs is worth their weight in gold. They stay invested in understanding the tax nuances of various professions and can provide priceless insights tailored to your specific business.

Networking with other solo entrepreneurs and business owners can lead to shared knowledge about tax law updates. Peer groups, online forums, and industry associations are excellent platforms where news and experiences are exchanged. Not only can you learn from others' experiences, but you can also gain different perspectives on how to handle tax changes.

Education is a powerful tool, and today's learning platforms offer an unending stream of resources. Tax law courses, webinars, and workshops built for small business owners can demystify updates in tax regulations and make them more digestible. A modest investment in continual learning can yield significant returns come tax time.

Be proactive in asking questions and seeking clarification whenever you come across terms or changes you don't fully understand. Whether it's a direct query to the IRS, a question posed in a seminar, or an email to your tax advisor, clarity is your best friend in the complex world of taxes.

Understand that state tax laws may change independently of federal laws and can carry just as many implications for your business finances. Staying informed on both levels is crucial, especially if you operate across state lines. Each state can have unique credits, deductions, and even deadlines that you need to be aware of.

Consider international tax law if your business operates across borders. Global tax regulations can change due to shifts in international relations, trade agreements, and economic policies. A global perspective is becoming increasingly important even for smaller-scale solo entrepreneurs who engage with foreign markets.

Use official tax seasons as an impromptu 'spring cleaning' time to refresh your knowledge on existing tax laws as well. While learning about new changes, revisit the old ones to ensure no details have slipped through the cracks. This helps maintain a strong foundation for understanding how newer updates interact with the existing tax framework.

Always document the source of your tax law updates. In an era of abundant information, ensuring that your knowledge comes from a reputable and accurate source cannot be overstated. This due diligence will protect you from relying on outdated or incorrect information that could have negative repercussions for your tax filings.

Embrace the routine of revision. Tax codes can often loop back on themselves, amending earlier language, or updating provisions that seemed settled. Keep your finger on the pulse of these revisions to ensure your tax strategies remain relevant and effective.

Consider the long-term implications of tax law changes on your business planning. Tax code updates can signal broader economic trends that could impact your business model, your retirement planning, and your growth strategies. By paying attention to the larger narrative, you can align your business with the trajectory of potential future tax landscapes.

Staying informed on tax law updates is not merely about legal compliance; it's a strategic business practice that shores up the vigor of your venture. Your awareness and adaptability in the face of tax law changes will not just save you from penalties, but can steer you towards greater prosperity and sustainability. Take ownership of this knowledge, and let it empower you to navigate the seas of solo entrepreneurship with confidence and clarity.

Adapting Your Tax Strategy to Legislative Changes

As a nimble solo entrepreneur, staying agile is part of your DNA. This flexibility isn't just about pivoting your business model or finding new niche markets—it extends to navigating the ever-shifting sands of tax laws. Perhaps you've already charted a course through the complexities of the tax system, but how do you keep your tax strategy afloat amidst legislative changes?

Let's start with a truth that many business owners come to learn the hard way: tax law is as mutable as the weather. Laws can change with the political winds, which makes keeping your tax strategy static a risky proposition. The trick is to not only weather these changes but use them to your advantage.

When new tax legislation is passed, it's like someone shuffled the deck you've been carefully arranging. Your first step is to lay out your cards again, by understanding how these changes affect your business. Grab the cheat sheets, summaries, or even the full text of the new laws—you're going to need them to play your next hand wisely.

Keep your eyes peeled for key changes that are relevant to your business structure. Are there new deductions or credits for LLCs, S Corps, or sole proprietorships? Has the self-employment tax landscape shifted in a way that needs a fresh approach to your estimated payments? These nuances matter, as they are your new rule book.

Change can bring opportunities. For instance, new tax reforms might introduce incentives for energy efficiency, which could be a boon if you're considering green upgrades to your office space. Another law might increase the cap on retirement contributions, allowing you to stash away more pre-tax dollars while shoring up your future security.

Tweaking your tax strategy requires a dose of creativity. If a new deduction is introduced, think about lawful ways to maximize it within your business operations. This is where your entrepreneurial spirit shines—you're adept at finding value where others might not even look.

One crucial aspect is timing. Legislative changes might come at a time when shifting income or expenses could be beneficial. For instance, if a new law reduces tax rates beginning next year, it might pay off to defer some income to take advantage of the lower rates.

Being proactive is key. Rather than scrambling to respond to tax law changes at tax time, integrate them into your ongoing financial management throughout the year. This way, when tax season arrives, you're not reactive; you're ready.

Keeping abreast of changes in laws can be daunting, but it's essential. Subscribe to newsletters, follow thought leaders in finance, and make a habit of scanning the headlines for tax news. A little bit of dedicated reading can pay dividends in preparedness.

Now, let's talk about your safety net—deductions. Each year, evaluate which deductions and credits are most beneficial to you, and make sure your record-keeping aligns with making those claims. With legislative changes, some deductions might become more valuable, while others might be phased out.

Consider technology as your co-pilot on this journey. Tax software and apps often update with the latest laws, reducing your chances of missing out on new advantages or running afoul of new requirements. Harness these tools to streamline your tax strategy and avoid potential pitfalls.

Be mindful that some legislative changes could call for a restructuring of your business entity. Perhaps the benefits of being a sole proprietor no longer outweigh the advantages of an S Corp status, given the new tax environment. Analyze, assess, and if necessary, adjust.

While technology and reading keep you on your toes, nothing replaces expert advice. A trusted tax professional can be an invaluable ally, decoding complex changes and helping tailor your strategy to take full advantage of new laws. Yes, it's an added expense, but think of it as investing in a smoother sail.

Lastly, embrace adaptability not just in your business model, but in your mindset. The tax landscape will always be a terrain of peaks and valleys, but with the right attitude, you can navigate it with the confidence of an explorer. Each new law is a path to potentially undiscovered savings or strategies. Your job is to chart a course and follow it through.

Remember, as a solo entrepreneur, you are the captain of your ship. Tax laws will come and go, but your ability to pivot and adapt is what truly defines your business's success and resilience. With a timely and strategic response to the inevitable winds of change in taxation, you'll continue to sail smoothly toward your financial goals.

Chapter 10:
Hiring Professionals:
When and How to Seek Expert Help

Success in the solo entrepreneurial journey isn't just about what you can do; it's equally about recognizing when you've hit a limit and need to call in reinforcements. Hiring a tax professional might feel like a leap, especially when you're used to steering the ship alone, but it's a strategic move that can pay dividends. It's about striking that delicate balance—understanding that while you're the maestro of your business, there are moments when the complexities of tax laws resemble a labyrinth best navigated with a guide. Knowing when to seek expert advice isn't a sign of weakness; think of it as a power move, a conscious decision to fortify your financial future and safeguard your business against the pitfalls of an ever-changing tax landscape. It's not just about crunching numbers; it's a partnership aimed at growing your business and preserving your energy for where it counts. In this chapter, we hone in on the triggers that signal it's time to bring a professional on board, explore the cost versus benefits, and provide actionable advice on finding someone who doesn't just crunch the numbers but also understands the heartbeat of your business.

Determining Whether You Need an Accountant or Tax Advisor

Embarking on the entrepreneurial journey means embracing the jack-of-all-trades role, but when it comes to taxes, even the sharpest of soloists can hit a wrong note. Consider this: taxes aren't just an annual ordeal—they weave into the daily fabric of your business operation. As the financial landscape becomes increasingly complex, it's essential to weigh the scale of your endeavors against your tax expertise. Do you find yourself spending more time deciphering tax codes than growing your business, or are you staying up at night pondering if you've seized every tax advantage at your disposal? It might be time to turn the page and seek harmony with a professional. An accountant or tax advisor can be the virtuoso you need to fine-tune your financial performance, ensuring you're not only compliant but also maximizing your hard-earned dollars. They're your front line of defense against overpayment and can spot tax-saving opportunities that might otherwise slip through the cracks. Deciding to hire one isn't an admission of defeat; it's a strategic move towards greater financial symphony and peace of mind.

Cost-Benefit Analysis of Professional Services As a self-reliant entrepreneur, you're accustomed to wearing multiple hats. However, when it comes to taxes, the decision to handle them solo or to enlist professional help can feel daunting. Let's navigate this terrain together by performing a thorough cost-benefit analysis of professional services to ensure you allocate your financial resources wisely.

Firstly, it's important to recognize that the time you spend on tax matters is time diverted from revenue-generating activities. Calculate the hours you anticipate spending on tax preparation and multiply them by your hourly rate. This gives you a baseline figure representing the opportunity cost of do-it-yourself (DIY) tax prep.

On the flip side, weigh the potential costs of professional services. Hiring a CPA or tax advisor could range from a few hundred to several thousand dollars, based on the complexity of your tax situation and the professional's expertise. Yet, don't simply look at this figure in isolation. Skilled professionals can often uncover tax savings opportunities and deductions that might otherwise be overlooked, possibly offsetting their fees.

Consider your stress levels and peace of mind in this equation. Taxes aren't just about crunching numbers; they involve intricate knowledge of the tax code, which is constantly evolving. A professional stays abreast of these changes and can advise you accordingly, allowing you to focus on your business with one less worry on your plate.

Let's not forget accuracy. Errors in tax filings can result in penalties and interest, or trigger an audit. These outcomes carry their own costs. A proficient tax professional will minimize the likelihood of such pitfalls, providing an additional financial safeguard.

The complexity of your tax situation is also a determining factor. If your business dealings are straightforward, a DIY approach may suffice. Yet, as your enterprise grows, involving variables like multi-state sales tax compliance, home office deductions, or retirement savings plans, the intricacies increase. Professional guidance in these scenarios could prove invaluable and financially judicious.

What about the long-term relationship benefits? Engaging with a tax professional is not a one-off transaction. It's a partnership where the professional gains intimate knowledge of your business over time. This understanding can lead to strategic tax planning that optimizes your financial outcomes in the years to come.

Audit representation is another critical advantage. Should the IRS come knocking, having a trusted professional who is already familiar with your financial landscape can be a game-changer. They can represent you and handle communications with the IRS, a service that is typically outside the purview of DIY tax software or non-professional assistance.

Additionally, deliberate on the learning curve and software costs if you opt for the DIY route. Tax software isn't always free, and there's invariably a learning curve associated with any new technology. Factor in these aspects to evaluate whether the DIY savings truly add up.

Don't underestimate the power of networking either. Tax professionals often belong to a network of other business services and can refer you to reliable professionals for other needs, such as legal advice or financial planning.

Another consideration is liability. Many tax professionals carry errors and omissions insurance. This means that if a mistake is made, the professional—not you—could bear the financial brunt of that error, reducing your risk exposure.

Many entrepreneurs view tax planning as a static chore – once a year and done. A reputable tax advisor sees the broader picture, offering advice that aligns your tax strategy with business goals, investment decisions, and personal financial planning.

In the end, your decision may boil down to personality and how you value control. If you enjoy meticulous record-keeping and have a knack for finance, you might prefer direct management of your tax affairs. Alternatively, if you view the tax process as a labyrinth best navigated by a seasoned guide, professional services will likely be more appealing.

Before making your choice, solicit quotes from various professionals. Ask about their experience with clients in your specific niche. Inquire about the full scope of their services and the value they'll add. Being armed with this information will help you make an informed decision.

Evaluate efficiency as well. If a professional can complete your taxes in a fraction of the time it takes you, even if you're knowledgeable in the area, this time saved can be redirected towards profitable activities within your business.

In conclusion, while the lure of saving money with a DIY approach to tax preparation is strong, it's essential to weigh it against the potential savings, increased accuracy, peace of mind, and other benefits that come from employing professional services. Reflect on the value of your time, the complexity of your tax situation, and the long-term advantages of building a relationship with a knowledgeable tax advisor. Your solo entrepreneurial journey need not be a solo voyage through the tumultuous seas of tax compliance—professionals can help you chart a course that maximizes favorable financial outcomes while keeping you compliant and focused on growing your business.

Tips for Finding and Working with a Tax Professional

As a solo entrepreneur, your time should be spent doing what you do best – running your business. When it comes time to navigate the complex waters of taxes, finding a knowledgeable tax professional is not just a smart move, it's essential to your financial health and business compliance. Here are some actionable tips to ensure you find and successfully collaborate with the right expert for your tax needs.

Start by recognizing that not all tax professionals are created equal. The term 'tax professional' is a broad one, encompassing certified public accountants (CPAs), enrolled agents (EAs), tax attorneys, and sometimes less-credentialed tax preparers. A CPA generally has a vast knowledge of accounting and can help you with overall financial strategy. EAs are experts in tax law and are the only professionals who can represent you before the IRS without limitation. Tax attorneys are essential if you're dealing with legal matters. Your specific situation will determine whom you should look for.

Referrals can be golden when it comes to finding a trustworthy tax pro. Ask fellow business owners, especially those in similar industries, for recommendations. These peers have likely faced similar tax situations and can point you towards someone with relevant experience. Look for professionals who are familiar with the nuances of tax issues faced by solo entrepreneurs.

Once you have a few names in hand, verify credentials. Ensure that whoever you're considering is licensed and in good standing, which can be checked through the respective state board or the IRS directory. Don't be shy to ask for references and to inquire about their professional affiliations, such as membership in the American Institute of Certified Public Accountants (AICPA) or the National Association of Enrolled Agents (NAEA).

After checking credentials, interview candidates. This is a critical step to assess not only their expertise but also their communication skills and compatibility with your working style. You want someone who is personable, understands your industry, and can explain tax concepts in a way that makes sense to you.

Discuss their approach to client communication. How often will they update you? What's their policy on responding to emails or phone calls? It's key to establish a clear line of communication from the outset to avoid frustration during critical times, such as the approach of tax deadlines or in the event of an IRS notice.

Enquire about their experience with the IRS should you ever face an audit. You want a tax professional who will stand by your side and has a successful track record of defending clients' tax positions.

Clarify fees upfront to avoid surprises. Rather than a vague notion of cost, ask for specific rates regarding annual tax preparation, audit representation, and any other services. Tax professionals should provide a clear fee structure; if not, it may be a red flag.

Ensure the tax professional is well-versed in the latest tax laws that pertain to your business. Tax codes change frequently, and you need someone agile enough to optimize your tax position while maintaining compliance. A proactive advisor will make suggestions to save money on taxes and avoid penalties.

It's also beneficial to find a tax professional who is tech-savvy. In today's digital age, efficient tax work often requires proficiencies in online accounting tools and secure file-sharing platforms. A tech-equipped expert can streamline processes and provide a better client experience.

Ask about the structure of their practice. Is your potential tax professional a solo practitioner, or do they work with a team? A team might provide more resources and expertise, but it's important to know who you will be primarily dealing with. Solo practitioners can give more personalized service, but may have limited bandwidth during peak times.

Assess their year-round availability. Some tax professionals work only during the tax season and may not be available for consultation during other times of the year. Find out if they are accessible beyond tax season as your business decision-making doesn't adhere to the IRS schedule.

Consider if they offer a holistic approach. Good tax advice should not be given in a vacuum. Ask if they are willing to work with your other financial advisors, such as financial planners or attorneys, which can result in more comprehensive advice.

Lastly, trust your instincts. You're entering a relationship that requires sharing confidential financial details. If you're not comfortable with the professional during your initial meetings, chances are the unease will continue. Compatibility is essential.

Finding the right tax professional might take some effort, but the peace of mind and potential savings you gain make it a worthwhile endeavor. Once you have found someone, nurture that relationship. A tax professional who really understands your business can become a valuable asset, aiding in your financial planning strategy for years to come.

In summary, don't overlook the importance of this decision. The right tax professional is a partner in your business growth and, when chosen wisely, is an investment that pays dividends in financial clarity, tax savings, and legal compliance. Take the time to do your research, ask the right questions, and make an informed choice that suits your unique tax needs.

Chapter 11:
Retirement and Exit Strategies for the Solo
Entrepreneur

As solo entrepreneurs, we juggle day-to-day operations with long-range planning, and all too often, retirement strategies might land on the back burner. But, laying the groundwork for a comfortable future is just as crucial as today's success. Harnessing the power of tax-deferred retirement accounts, you're not only preparing for a sunny future but also reducing your taxable income in the present—a double win. When the time comes to bid farewell to your business, knowing the ins and outs of seller financing, capital gains, and business valuation can be as empowering as getting your first client. A solid exit strategy should seamlessly integrate into your retirement plans, ensuring a smooth and financially sound transition. And don't fret over complexity; a well-conceived plan, built step by step, can lead to an exit as successful as the empire you've built. This chapter is your compass to navigating the turning point every entrepreneur eventually faces—shifting from the driver's seat to a well-deserved spot in the sun.

Tax-Efficient Retirement Planning

Embarking on the journey of retirement planning as a solo entrepreneur brings its own set of challenges and opportunities. Key to mastering this process is embracing tax-efficient strategies that align with your business and personal retirement goals. Balancing the immediate benefits of deductions today with the long-term rewards of a secure retirement tomorrow requires insight, planning, and a sharp eye for detail.

As a solo entrepreneur, you have the unique opportunity to tailor retirement plans to your specific needs. The several retirement savings vehicles at your disposal, such as SEP-IRAs, SIMPLE IRAs, and Solo 401(k) plans each offer distinct advantages. Your mission is to identify the right mix that offers both tax deferral and the flexibility your entrepreneurial life demands.

Start with a self-evaluation, considering your current income, projected growth, and desired retirement lifestyle. Keep in mind that tax deferral isn't just about postponing taxes but also potentially reducing your overall tax burden if you expect to be in a lower tax bracket in retirement. Evaluating your current tax bracket is essential in identifying how much you would benefit from tax deductions now versus tax deferral for later.

SEP-IRAs are a favorite for many solo entrepreneurs due to their high contribution limits and simplicity. Funding a SEP-IRA can significantly reduce your taxable income each year. However, keep in mind that contribution limits are tied to your self-employment earnings, which can vary year to year based on the success of your business.

A SIMPLE IRA might be the right fit if your business is on the smaller side or you have a few employees. These plans are relatively easy to set up and maintain, and they allow for both employer and employee contributions, offering a bit of flexibility depending on your business's profitability.

For those looking for the highest possible contribution limits, the Solo 401(k) plan might be the perfect match. This type of plan also offers loan provisions and the possibility for after-tax contributions, which can grow tax-free if certain conditions are met. A Solo 401(k) plan can be a powerful tool, but it generally requires more management than SEP or SIMPLE IRAs.

It's important to remember that while contributing to any retirement plan reduces your current taxable income, you'll pay taxes on distributions in retirement. However, if structured correctly, the tax rate on these future distributions could be lower than your current tax rate, ensuring overall tax savings.

Another key element in tax-efficient retirement planning is understanding how to manage taxable income in retirement. Withdrawals from your retirement accounts will typically count as taxable income. Hence, planning how and when to take these distributions can help minimize your tax hit during retirement.

Tapping into accounts like Roth IRAs, which offer tax-free withdrawals, can be a smart strategy as part of your retirement income plan. While Roth accounts don't provide an immediate tax benefit, the back-end rewards could be substantial, especially if tax rates rise in the future or if your retirement income is higher than anticipated.

Health savings accounts (HSAs) can also play a role in your tax-efficiency plan. Contributions are tax-deductible, and funds can grow tax-free and be withdrawn tax-free for qualified medical expenses. After age 65, you can use the funds for any purpose without penalty, although withdrawals for non-medical expenses are taxable.

Diversification extends beyond investment selections. Diversifying your retirement income streams across different tax treatments can provide flexibility in managing your tax burden. Having a mix of taxable, tax-deferred, and tax-free accounts gives you levers to pull to help manage your income and taxes each year in retirement.

Entrepreneurs should also consider the timing of retirement contributions. If you're experiencing a high-income year, maximizing contributions may provide immediate tax relief. If it's a lower-income year, you might consider contributing less to retirement accounts, keeping more cash available for business needs.

Don't forget to re-evaluate your retirement planning whenever your life circumstances or tax laws change. Tax laws evolve, businesses grow or contract, and personal lives shift, all potentially impacting your optimal retirement planning strategy.

Finally, stay vigilant about the ever-present risk of penalties. Failing to take required minimum distributions or withdrawing funds too early can lead to penalties. Understanding these rules will help maintain the integrity of your retirement planning.

The allocation of time, effort, and resources today towards a tax-efficient retirement strategy is akin to planting a garden. With the right mix of soil (tax-advantaged accounts), seeds (contributions), and care (planning), you can cultivate a bountiful future harvest that sustains you through your retirement years. Ensure you leverage the tax code to your benefit, creating a nest egg that not only allows you to retire comfortably but also efficiently manages your tax obligations.

Selling Your Business: Tax Considerations and Strategies

So, you're thinking about selling your business. Whether it's because you're eyeing a relaxing retirement or the idea of starting a new chapter excites you, it's a huge step that requires careful planning—especially where taxes are involved. The impact of taxes on the sale can significantly alter the amount you walk away with, so let's dive into some key considerations and strategies you can use to handle this transition smoothly.

First things first, understanding the structure of your business is crucial. Is your enterprise an LLC, S Corp, or sole proprietorship? Each structure carries different tax implications for a sale. For individual proprietors, the sale often means dealing with capital gains taxes—your profit from the sale is subject to taxation. Planning for capital gains tax efficiently could mean timing the sale or structuring payment terms in a way that keeps you from a higher tax bracket bump.

Now, let's talk about the allocation of sale price. When selling, the total price is usually allocated among assets like equipment, inventory, goodwill, and other intangible property. You'll want to strategize this with an eye on tax consequences since different types of assets may be taxed at different rates. For instance, the sale of tangible assets might be taxed as ordinary income, while intangible assets, like goodwill, benefit from lower capital gains rates. Work with a professional to allocate the sale price in a tax-advantageous way.

Another critical strategy involves tax deferral. Instead of getting the entire payment upfront, consider an installment sale where you receive the payments over a period of years. This approach can spread out your taxable income and potentially keep you in a lower tax bracket each year. However, remember that there are trade-offs, including seller-financing risks and the fact that tax rates could change in the future.

Capital improvements you've made over the years might be your ticket to tax savings. If you've upgraded equipment or your workspace, these improvements may reduce your capital gains. It's all about calculating your adjusted basis—what you've invested in your business property, which includes the cost of improvements.

Depreciation recapture is another matter you shouldn't overlook. If you've claimed depreciation on assets over the years, Uncle Sam will want a piece of that pie back when you sell. Recaptured depreciation is taxed as ordinary income, not at the typically lower capital gains rate. Careful planning can help minimize this tax bite, possibly by using like-kind exchanges or similar strategies.

A potential landmine is the dreaded inventory tax. If you have an inventory, the amount you receive for it is taxed as ordinary income. It's basic but often overlooked—don't conflate inventory sales with asset sales; they're different beasts in the tax world.

If you've established a more complex entity structure like an S Corp, then you're looking at different scenarios. S Corporations have the advantage of avoiding double taxation, but the IRS watches closely for built-in gains—a tax on appreciation of assets that occurred before you converted to S Corp status. Again, understanding your entity and its history is indispensable.

Thinking about the tax implications before you sign on the dotted line is vital. This isn't just about taxes you'll pay today but also about your long-term financial health. Don't forget state taxes, either. Depending on where your business is located, there could be state-level income taxes or even franchise tax considerations for the sale.

One strategic move you may want to consider is gifting portions of your business to heirs prior to the sale. This can reduce your tax liability and leverage gift and estate tax exemptions. Of course, this requires planning ahead and an understanding of current tax laws that influence gifting.

Get your timing right. Taxes aren't just about dollars; they're also about dates. Year-end sales might push you into a higher tax bracket for that year—could selling in January keep more money in your pocket? It's a question for the calendars and calculators, and one worth asking.

Don't ignore the power of retirement plan contributions. If you've been savvy with SEP-IRA, SIMPLE IRA, or Solo 401(k) plans, you might be able to cushion the tax blow by contributing to your retirement accounts. Maxing out contributions in the sale year could effectively reduce taxable income.

In all cases, it's paramount to have an excellent team in your corner. This is not the time to go DIY on your taxes. A trusted accountant or tax advisor, who gets the ins and outs of business sales, becomes worth their weight in gold—helping you navigate complex tax legislation, spot deductions you might miss, and strategize for both immediate and future tax implications.

Don't entertain the idea that once the sale is closed, your tax considerations are done. Often, post-sale audits happen when the IRS suspects underreported income or overreported deductions from the sale. Keep your documentation pristine, and maintain those records well beyond the sale to ensure you're covered if the IRS comes knocking.

Last but not least, remember, the sale of your business isn't just a transaction; it's a pivotal moment in your entrepreneurial journey. With the right tax strategies in place, you're setting yourself up for the next adventure, be it retirement or new business ventures. Your financial savviness today can ensure that when you turn the page, you're not leaving money on the table for the taxman—but securing it for your future dreams.

Chapter 12:
Advanced Tax Strategies for the
Seasoned Entrepreneur

B y now, you've got the tax basics down pat, and your entrepreneurial gears are finely tuned to the rhythm of regular record-keeping and compliance. But there's a world of tax strategy that goes beyond the basics, designed to propel the savvy entrepreneur into realms of significant savings and fiscal finesse. In this vital chapter, we're delving deep into the finer points of tax tactics that'll have you nodding along in agreement – because let's face it, you're beyond ready to explore the full potential of S Corporations, to unearth the jewels of advanced retirement plans, and to master the art of deferring taxes like a seasoned chess player. It's about leveraging every legal avenue to ensure that your hard-earned profits are shielded smartly, ensuring more of your revenue is reinvested in the growth and longevity of your business. We're not just scratching the surface; we're mining the depths of knowledge that can transform tax from a chore into a strategic advantage. So let's gear up to navigate through the sophisticated landscape of tax planning that could very well redefine the horizon of your entrepreneurial success.

Utilizing S Corporations for Tax Savings

Transitioning into the realm of S corporations can seem daunting, but it's akin to finding a hidden pathway in the labyrinth of taxation that leads to a treasure trove of savings. The seasoned entrepreneur, with eyes fixed on financial efficiency, might just find that electing an S Corporation status for their business is a strategic move worthy of serious consideration.

The magic of an S Corporation lies in how it blends the legal protection of a corporation with the tax advantages of a pass-through entity. By filing Form 2553 with the IRS, your business could steer clear of the double tax hit that plagues classic C Corporations. This move allows the business's profits–and losses–to pass directly to shareholders without incurring corporate tax levels.

Now, why is all that important? Well, imagine being able to legitimately reduce self-employment taxes, which often gnaw away at the your hard-earned profits. Normally as a sole proprietor, you're required to pay these taxes on your entire net income. But as an S Corp, you can wear two hats – that of an owner and an employee. As an employee, you draw a reasonable salary, which means you only pay self-employment taxes on that salary, not on the entire profits of the company.

Walking this path does not come without its pebbles and stones. S Corps demand meticulous payroll processing, reasonable compensation analysis, and adherence to shareholder guidelines. If these tasks seem onerous, remember the potential savings that await on the other side.

Moreover, the profits that exceed your salary aren't subject to Medicare and Social Security taxes. This can mean a tangible cut in your tax liabilities. However, the keyword here is 'reasonable'. The IRS is keen to ensure that S Corp owners are paid a fair market salary for their role. Anything less, and you might just wave a red flag that beckons an IRS audit.

In the context of maximizing tax savings, it's pivotal to balance your salary against distributions. Tip the scales too far in favor of low salary and high distributions, and you'll stand out in the IRS's eyes. The goal is to find that sweet spot where you can justify your compensation while maximizing your distributions, thus optimizing your tax position.

Let's dive into benefits that may not be immediately obvious. With an S Corporation, you can smoothly make a transition to a more traditional retirement plan, which can afford you higher contribution limits compared to those available to sole proprietors. This means not only saving for the future but doing so in a tax-efficient manner.

Another hidden gem with S Corporations is the favorable treatment of fringe benefits. Shareholders who own less than 2% of the company can treat benefits like health insurance as a deductible business expense, providing further tax relief and contributing to your overall financial strategy.

To navigate these waters effectively, it is wise to employ solid accounting practices. S Corporations require separate bank accounts, distinct accounting records, and regular financial statements, solidifying the corporate veil and reinforcing your business's credibility in the eyes of the law.

Speaking of law, don't forget the state implications of having an S Corporation. Each state views S Corporations differently in terms of tax treatment. While most honor the federal disregard for corporate income taxation, some do not. It's crucial, therefore, to understand your state's stand on S Corps and to align your strategies accordingly.

As for the administrative burden, yes, there's more paperwork involved, including the infamous shareholder meetings and keeping of minutes. While it might feel cumbersome, view it as a rite of passage—a structured approach that brings discipline and could very well save your bacon if the IRS comes knocking.

Before jumping the gun, it makes sense to consult with a tax professional. Whether an S Corporation is the right fit for you depends on your business specifics, your income level, and your long-term goals. It's not a one-size-fits-all situation, and expert advice is invaluable in tailoring a strategy that suits your unique circumstances.

Should you decide to go down this path, timing plays a critical role. The IRS allows you to make the S Corp election by March 15 of the tax year. A stitch in time here could secure financial benefits for the whole year. Procrastination, on the other hand, could delay the advantages only to the following year.

In conclusion, utilizing an S Corporation for tax savings is akin to a chess game. Play your moves strategically—with a strong understanding of regulations, expert advice at your side, and an eye towards future benefits—and you're likely to solidify your winning position in the great game of business tax optimization.

Remember, tax mastery isn't about evasion; it's about wise navigation of the laws in place. With an S Corporation, you're not just a business owner; you're a savvy architect of your financial future, leveraging the structures available to craft a tax-efficient path forward.

Advanced Retirement Plans and Tax Deferral Techniques

As you venture deeper into the world of entrepreneurship, attention must shift to the future and retirement. Advanced retirement planning is not just about stashing away money; it's a strategic move to reduce your current tax burden and secure your financial independence down the road. Let's explore the tax-advantageous retirement vehicles and deferral methods that seasoned solopreneurs can leverage.

First off, consider the potential of a Solo 401(k), especially if you don't have employees. This retirement plan allows for significant pretax contributions as both employee and employer, giving you a considerable tax deduction and the ability to grow your savings tax-deferred. In 2023, the total contribution can be quite substantial when you total employee and employer limits.

Another sophisticated option is the Simplified Employee Pension Plan, or SEP-IRA. This vehicle is beloved for its high contribution limits and flexibility in annual contributions, making it ideal if your business income varies from year to year. You get to adjust your contributions accordingly and reduce taxable income significantly in the process.

You might also want to look into a Defined Benefit Plan. This is particularly effective if you're a bit closer to retirement age and need to catch up. These plans can promise a set annual benefit upon retirement, and as a result, they permit much larger contributions. The catch is they come with complexity and require actuarial calculations, but the tax savings can be immense.

Now, for those with a bit more risk appetite, Cash Balance Plans are an intriguing hybrid. They blend some characteristics of defined benefit and defined contribution plans. With higher potential contribution limits than a Solo 401(k), they can significantly decrease your tax bill and amass wealth for retirement in a comparatively shorter timeframe.

The beauty of all these plans is not only in the present tax benefits but in the power of tax deferral. As your investments within these plans grow, they won't be subject to tax until you withdraw them, often in retirement when you may be in a lower tax bracket. This can result in a substantial difference in the accumulated wealth over time.

One often overlooked tool is a Health Savings Account (HSA). If you have a high-deductible health plan, you can contribute to an HSA with pretax dollars, and these funds can be used for eligible medical expenses tax-free. But what's exciting for entrepreneurs eyeing long-term growth is that HSAs can also be used as a retirement vehicle where funds can grow tax-free, adding another layer to your strategic tax planning.

Let's not forget Roth options. Although a Roth IRA or Roth 401(k) doesn't provide an immediate tax deduction, they offer tax-free growth and withdrawals in retirement. There may be income limits for these, but backdoor Roth conversions might be an avenue to explore for higher earners.

Asset location is another savvy strategy. It involves placing investments within your retirement accounts that are expected to generate high taxable income or short-term gains, thus benefiting from the tax-deferred growth. Simultaneously, holding more tax-efficient investments, like long-term capital gains assets, in taxable accounts can also capitalize on lower tax rates.

Consider also non-discrimination tests for certain plans. If your business grows and you start hiring employees, you'll want to ensure that your retirement plan is compliant with IRS rules that prevent discrimination in favor of highly compensated employees, including yourself. This will require a balance between optimizing contributions for yourself and offering a fair plan for your employees.

An often-overlooked element is succession planning. As you plan for retirement, also think about the eventual transition of your business. A well-structured retirement plan can be an asset during a business sale, potentially providing ongoing income or preferential tax treatment for the proceeds.

Advanced retirement planning is part art, part science. It requires a strong grasp of the tax code, foresight, and a willingness to adjust as circumstances evolve. Keep in mind, the tax landscape isn't static, and what works one year might not be as advantageous the next. Part of strategic tax planning is staying adaptive and informed.

When considering these advanced retirement plans, it's also beneficial to model different scenarios to determine the optimal contributions and tax deferral techniques based on your projected income, savings goal, and retirement timeline. This will often require consultations with a tax professional or financial planner who can provide personalized advice tailored to your unique situation.

To wrap the topic, advanced retirement plans and tax deferral techniques aren't just a matter of stowing away funds; they are about creating a comprehensive and adaptable approach to reducing your tax liability, accelerating your savings, and securing your future financial freedom. With the right strategy, the later years of your entrepreneurship can be just as prosperous as your most profitable quarters, ensuring that you transition into retirement on your terms—financially confident and secure.

Remember, your journey as a solo entrepreneur is one punctuated by many decisions, and how you plan for retirement can have lasting implications. Approach your advanced tax strategy not just with numbers in mind but with the vision of the lifestyle you wish to lead, and let that drive your planning forward.

Chapter 13:
Taking Control of Your Taxes and Your Future

You've delved deep into the intricacies of tax law, dissected the nuances of various business structures, and scrutinized best practices for record-keeping and deductions. But as we bring this guide to a close, it's time to focus on the bigger picture: how grasping the reins of your tax strategy can empower you to envisage and sculpt the future you aspire to.

Control may seem like a lofty word when dealing with something as complex and fickle as taxes, yet it's precisely what you gain when you apply the knowledge you've acquired. By understanding the tax system, you ensure that your hard-earned money is serving your long-term goals instead of being lost to preventable mistakes or inefficiency.

Each chapter of this journey has built upon the last to create a comprehensive strategy tailored for solo entrepreneurs like yourself. We've covered the spectrum from elementary concepts to intricate strategies, ensuring that every reader—whether novice or seasoned—finds value they can apply immediately to their business.

An entrepreneur's relationship with taxes doesn't have to be adversarial. By maximizing deductions and credits, leveraging the right business structure, and hiring professionals judiciously, you can convert what feels like an obligation into a valuable tool for business growth. Keep tabs on changes in the tax law—what may seem like a mere update could present fresh opportunities to save or even make money.

Remember, tax planning is not just about this year, but about the trajectory of your enterprise. Nurturing a future-proof strategy—a blend of smart record-keeping, astute planning, and judicious professional help—can alleviate financial strain and germinate the seeds of enduring prosperity.

What's more, adopting a proactive approach to your taxes can unshackle you from the yearly stress that comes with deadlines and scrambling for documents. Instead, you'll find that the continual process of being on top of your financial situation can bolster your peace of mind.

Practicality aside, there's a certain pride in self-reliance that comes with managing your taxes well. When you make astute tax decisions, you're not just saving money; you're taking a stand for your business's integrity and your personal values. This kind of empowerment is critical as you continue to carve a unique path in the world of business.

And don't forget, while the landscape may shift—whether due to new legislation or life changes—the principles you've learned here are robust. Stay agile, keep learning, and maintain a responsiveness to change that befits the dynamic world of the solo entrepreneur.

Let's not shy away from acknowledging the elephant in the room: taxes can be overwhelming. But, just like a daunting project or a massive business goal, they can be conquered by breaking them down into manageable, bite-sized pieces. This methodical approach will not only make tax management feasible but also far less intimidating.

Whether it's about determining the value of a tax professional or embarking upon advanced strategies for the more experienced entrepreneur, the key lies in understanding that taxes are a critical part of your business ecosystem. When managed well, they can significantly enhance your business's financial health.

Envision the future—a future where you are the master composer and taxes are just one of the instruments in your business symphony. Next year, when tax season rolls around, you'll find yourself anticipating it with savvy readiness rather than trepidation.

Finally, remember that taxes aren't just about laws and numbers—they're about people and their dreams. Your dream of being a successful solo entrepreneur isn't just about excelling in your craft but also about mastering the realms that support it, taxes included.

So, as you close this book and return to the hustle and bustle of your entrepreneurial life, carry with you the knowledge and confidence that you have what it takes to take control of your taxes. And by doing so, you take a firmer grasp on your future and all the promise it holds.

Go ahead, embrace the challenges, continue educating yourself, and apply the strategies you've found to be most effective. You're not just running a business; you're cultivating a lifestyle, a legacy that can stand firm in the face of shifting financial winds.

Your journey with taxes, much like your journey in business, is ongoing. But with each step, you're becoming more adept, more self-assured, and yes, more in control. Here's to your continuing success—in business, in taxes, and in life.

Appendix A:
Tax Resources and Tools for Solo Entrepreneurs

Tackling taxes as a solo entrepreneur doesn't have to feel like you're braving the wilderness without a compass. With each new chapter of your entrepreneurial journey, it's essential to have a reliable set of resources and tools at your disposal. The right information and applications not only streamline the tax process but also empower you to handle your obligations with confidence, all while sniffing out opportunities to save some hard-earned cash.

Let's dive into some invaluable resources and tools that can be a game-changer in managing your solo expedition through the tax landscape.

Government Resources

IRS for Small Business and Self-Employed: The official website for the IRS offers a treasure trove of information, including tax forms, instructional videos, and detailed guides tailored for the self-employed.

Small Business Administration (SBA): The SBA provides robust advice on planning, launching, managing, and growing your business, with an emphasis on the legal and financial aspects.

U.S. Department of Labor: For understanding your responsibilities as an employer (if you have employees), including tax implications and reporting requirements.

Accounting Software

Selecting the right accounting software is like choosing the best travel buddy—it should complement your work style and keep you organized. Consider features like expense tracking, mileage tracking, invoicing capabilities, and easy tax report generation.

QuickBooks Self-Employed: Tailor-made for freelancers and independent contractors, it comes with tax-specific features to help categorize expenses and estimate quarterly taxes.

Wave: An excellent budget-friendly option with free core services, suitable for sole proprietors who need basic accounting tools.

FreshBooks: Known for its user-friendly interface and excellent customer service, it's perfect for those who send out recurring invoices and want to accept credit card payments directly.

Tax Preparation Software

When it's time to file, tax prep software can make the job much less daunting. Just ensure the software caters to the self-employed, guiding you through deductions and credits while maximizing your returns.

TurboTax Self-Employed: Offers personalized guidance for industry-specific deductions and includes a feature for searching over 350 deductions.

H&R Block Premium & Business: Provides tools for the self-employed and small business owners, including guidance on asset depreciation and expense categorization.

Online Communities and Forums

You're not alone in this quest. There are vibrant online communities of fellow solo entrepreneurs where you can ask questions, share experiences, and find moral support.

Certain subreddits and LinkedIn groups focus on side hustles and self-employment.

Places like the QuickBooks Community offer forums where you can interact with tax experts and other business owners.

Educational Tools

It's vital to keep learning and stay on top of tax changes that might affect your business:

Regularly read blogs and articles from reputable tax and small business websites.

Enroll in webinars and online courses about small business taxation.

Subscribe to e-newsletters from tax professionals for updates and tips.

The resources and tools highlighted here are just the tip of the iceberg. They're starting points to build up your tax toolkit. As you grow your business, you'll find that pairing these resources with customized advice from a tax professional will serve you well. Your solo business is unique, and that means your tax journey is too. Embrace the available resources, and you'll not only navigate the tax seas with ease but also discover opportunities to bolster your finances, paving the way for a thriving business future.

Glossary of Tax Terms for Solo Entrepreneurs

As we navigate the various chapters of understanding and mastering tax obligations, it's crucial to have a clear grasp of the language used when dealing with taxes. This glossary will serve as a tool to demystify tax terms, helping you, the solo entrepreneur, to confidently tackle your tax planning and obligations. Keep this handy as you explore the depths of tax law and leverage it to empower your financial decisions.

Adjusted Gross Income (AGI)

Your total income after certain deductions, such as retirement plan contributions and student loan interest. This number is pivotal as it impacts your taxable income and eligibility for certain tax credits.

Audit

An official inspection of an individual's or organization's accounts, typically by the IRS, to ensure information is reported correctly according to tax laws.

Business Expense

Costs incurred in the ordinary course of business. These can often be deducted to lower taxable income, as long as they are both ordinary and necessary.

Capital Gains

The profit from the sale of assets such as stocks, bonds, or real estate. Capital gains tax rates can differ significantly from regular income tax rates.

Depreciation

A method to allocate the cost of tangible assets over their useful lives. It's a way of deducting the wear and tear on business property, like equipment or vehicles.

Estimated Tax Payments

Quarterly payments made to the IRS by individuals who expect to owe tax of $1,000 or more. This is common for solo entrepreneurs who don't have taxes withheld from a regular paycheck.

Form 1040-ES

A form used to calculate and submit estimated tax payments to the IRS.

IRS (Internal Revenue Service)

The government agency responsible for tax collection and tax law enforcement in the U.S.

Pass-Through Taxation

A tax structure of certain businesses, like sole proprietorships and S corporations, where earnings are passed through to the owners' personal tax returns, and business income is taxed at personal tax rates.

Quarterly Taxes

See Estimated Tax Payments.

Schedule C

A form used by sole proprietors to report income or loss from a business.

Self-Employment Tax

A tax covering Social Security and Medicare for individuals who work for themselves. It's similar to the Social Security and Medicare taxes withheld from the pay of most wage earners.

Sole Proprietorship

The simplest business form under which one can operate a business. It is not a legal entity and simply refers to a person who owns the business and is personally responsible for its debts.

Standard Deduction

A fixed amount that reduces the income you're taxed on. For 2021, the standard deduction is $12,550 for single filers and $25,100 for married couples filing jointly.

Tax Bracket

Ranges of income set by the IRS to determine the rate at which income is taxed. The higher your income, the higher the percentage you will pay on your top dollars earned.

Tax Deduction

An expense that can be subtracted from taxable income. Common deductions for solo entrepreneurs include business-related expenses, home office deductions, and self-employment taxes.

Tax Liability

The total amount of tax debt owed by an individual, corporation, or other entity to a taxing authority, like the IRS. It's the total amount of tax you're responsible for paying.

Understanding these terms is an essential step toward mastering your taxes and shaping a more robust financial future for yourself and your business. Keep advancing through the terrain of entrepreneurship with confidence, knowing that you're equipped with the knowledge to navigate the twists and turns of the tax world.

Appendix B:
Tax Organization Checklist

Tax time doesn't have to be a frantic scramble if you've got your ducks in a row throughout the year. The key to peace of mind - and a smoother tax filing experience - is organization. This checklist ensures you're ticking all the right boxes, so when tax season rolls around, you're not caught off guard.

Personal Information

Your Social Security Number (SSN) or Individual Taxpayer Identification Number (ITIN)

Spouse's SSN or ITIN and dates of birth for you and your spouse (if applicable)

Dependent information (if applicable)

Income Documents

All 1099 forms (MISC, INT, DIV, etc.) showing various types of income

Records of any other income not reported on 1099 forms, such as rent received, etc.

Bank and financial institution statements

Expense Records

Receipts for business expenses (categorized for ease)

Home office expenses (if applicable)

Vehicle use logs for business purposes and associated expenses

Records of estimated tax payments made

Deductions

Receipts for charitable contributions

Medical and healthcare payments

Property tax and mortgage interest statements

Education expenses and student loan interest statements

Retirement Contributions

Traditional and Roth IRA contributions

Statements from SEP-IRA, SIMPLE IRA, or Solo 401(k) plans

Health Insurance

Form 1095-A if you purchased insurance through the Marketplace

Records of premiums paid for private health insurance

Medical Savings Account (MSA) contributions

Business Records

Current year's profit and loss statement

Balance sheet

Payroll reports (if you have employees)

Inventory counts and asset purchase details

Sales Tax and Use Tax Records

Statements of sales tax collected

Receipts for major purchases and use tax calculations

Records Pertaining to Assets

Home purchase or closing statements

Investment or rental property purchase documents

Receipts for capital improvements to properties

Previous Year's Tax Information

Copy of the previous year's tax return

Notices or correspondence from the IRS or other tax agencies

It's natural to feel a bit overwhelmed with so much to track, but you're carving a path to success by staying organized. And you aren't just laying the groundwork for effectiveness during tax season, you're reinforcing robust habits that contribute to the overall health of your business. Keep in mind, this checklist is a starting point tailored to you, the mighty solo entrepreneur - use it as your foundation and customize as your business evolves. Consistency in staying on top of these items will not only simplify your tax process but will empower you to make savvy business and tax decisions throughout the year.

Every document, every receipt, and every log you keep adds up. They're not just pieces of paper or digital files; they're the building blocks of your financial fortitude and peace of mind. Now, with this checklist in hand, step boldly forward! Taxes don't stand a chance of catching you unprepared. And in this dance of numbers and forms, you're leading the way with confidence. Go ahead and take control of your taxes, and by extension, your future.